TO THE NATIONS FOR THE EARTH

TO THE NATIONS FOR THE EARTH

A MISSIONAL SPIRITUALITY

CHARLES FENSHAM

Clements Academic
Toronto, Ontario

Clements Publishing Group Inc.
6021 Yonge Street, Box 213
Toronto, Ontario M2M 3w2 Canada
www.clementspublishing.com

Cover image by Alexander Fensham. Used by permission.

Unless otherwise noted, Scripture quotations are taken from The New American Standard Bible®, copyright ©1960, 1962, 1963, 1968, 1971, 1972, 1973, 1975, 1977, 1995 by The Lockman Foundation. Used by permission.

A cataloguing record for this publication is available from Library and Archives Canada

ISBN 978-1-926798-09-7 (paper)
ISBN 978-1-926798-37-0 (electronic)

Contents

Acknowledgements

Joyful thankfulness expresses the very core of Christian spirituality. In this project I have so much to be thankful for and so many to thank! First to my family, my wonderful sons Alexander and Andrew, my Mom Yvonne, and sisters Marianthe and Therese I owe the debt of gratitude for their love and support. Friendship is a profound gift of grace and to my many friends, especially to Beth, Pam, Derek and Todd, Eric, Terence, John-Peter and Tori I offer thanks for ongoing encouragement and a willing ear to listen when my patience ran thin.

To my colleagues at Knox College and our Principal Dorcas Gordon I owe a special word of thanks. The wonderful opportunity to present my work to Faculty during our in house colloquia challenged me to think in new ways. Brian Irwin took some extra time and patiently helped me think better about the Hebrew text, Andrew Irvine spent many hours on the commute listening to my rants, all gave helpful feedback! Thanks must also be expressed to the Board of Governors of Knox College that supported me on Sabbatical to work on this project. The Faculty of Theology of the University of Western Cape, Cape Town, South Africa deserves special mention for their gift of spending time with them to bounce these ideas around and for their enriching perspectives into the Hebrew and Greek texts of the Bible and the perspective of cultural diversity and ecological accountability offered me under the leadership of Ernst Conradie.

My students are what it is all about, their reading and feedback of drafts kept me humble and my feet on the ground. The doctoral work of Dr. Bryan Lee on Moltmann's ecological theology, and Dr. Janet Chan on Barth and theological anthropology provided extra sharpness to my own thinking. A special word of thanks go to Matt Ruttan and his band of colleagues in ministry that read the first draft and provided helpful feedback. Rev. Beth McCutcheon took valuable vacation time to read a draft of this book and then sat down with me to talk it through. Thanks Beth! I also have to mention in a very special way Rob Clements who agreed to take on the re-publication of my previous book and this one as well. Rob's support and the exceptional work done by Clements Academic in supporting projects like this is a true labour of love. My own worshipping community, St. Mark's Presbyterian Church in Ontario and many friends in The Metropolitan Community Church of Toronto also walked with me in worship, prayer and love. They continue to challenge me to prac-

tice what I preach about diversity and listening. Above all, thanks be to God!
May we all walk the Way.

Prelude: The Song of the Universe

it began before time began
the One who is before
spoke
the dark void
shaped
by the Spirit order
all things out of giving Light
thus came the Call that creates our destiny

Thomas Berry and many others are right. We need to live out of a big story on our little globe floating through the unfathomable vastness of creation. Berry and Swimme have worked on their "Universe Story" to create a way for humankind to live sustainably and with love in our vulnerable biosphere[1]. They are right in this way – only a very big story, a story that gives us identity and calls us to our destiny as humankind will do. This book is about a Judeao-Christian, and particularly a Christian vision of this big story. It is my contention that we as Christian communities need to live out of such a theological vision that will inform our identity, and will inspire us towards our destiny. Only with such a grasp of the very nature of God as our Creator, and with the moral vision to live on the earth and within the Universe as vulnerable creatures, will we find a path to living right, well, and sustainably. In this Karl Barth's statement from his lecture 'Kriegszeit und Gottesreich' in 1915 was correct "World remains world, God is God."[2] For humankind to know its place, its limitations, and its creaturely state before God and within creation is critical.

As long as we run on the Enlightenment arrogance and the assumptions of the Industrial Revolution, as long as we consider ourselves as "masters and possessors" of creation, as Descartes put it, we are on a perilous journey to self destruction and we are violators of the sacred relationship between Creator and creatures. Even imagining ourselves as "co-creators", when taken arrogantly, risks threatening a proper understanding of who we are. Our place is more humble. We are caregivers to creation, a task we should engage with intelligence and all the innovative precociousness and creativeness of the human condition, but we are never creators in the final sense of the word. Even the latest claims by Craig Venter and his team of scientists that they are creating "life" by

1

putting some elements of creation together, vastly overstates what was actually achieved[3]. What they have done with $40 million in funding is scientifically impressive, yet the arrogance of the claim that they "created" life, and their apparent blindness to the foolhardiness of such a claim, is a symptom of what is wrong with our world.

We need to grasp and live out of a fundamental distinction between us as creatures and God as Creator. This is not the traditional distinction of dualism which has been harmful, but rather the distinction of place in the universe. We need to distinguish ourselves as in God and of God as opposed to being a kind of godpower ourselves. What is particularly Christian about the argument in this book and the way it tells the big story of God and creation is that this story involves the physical body of the Messiah. It is this body that establishes and merges the Divine and human in a particular way. The man Jesus' truly human state in history and time, his very physicality and its profound implications for our identity as human beings is part of the story. Indeed, it is a critical part of the story. Matter matters. Creation matters. Our destiny is not focused on an ethereal disembodied spirituality, but rather living in creation with all its embodied life. All of this life, we say with the Apostle Paul and the ancient Greek poet, is IN God (Acts 17:28).

We need to live out of the big story. If this is true, then our formation as people, and our formation for Christian spirituality need to arise out of this story as well. We need to start in the story and always return to it as our basic point of reference – our most fundamental sense of who we are. Therefore this book is about that story and the formation of people on a journey with God and creation. It is about the big story and its elements that shape our lives, our meaning – our destiny. This book is therefore about a theology of formation – a logic by which we grow to understand who we are and what constitutes us as people. As a theology of formation rooted in the big story of God and God's creation it strives to unfold the different dimensions of the big story in relation to the journey of being human over five chapters. These five chapters reflect the Christian tradition of worship which we call doxology.

Our humble place in relation to God as Creator means that God is not first of all our object of study or even enquiry; we are before God as creatures first of all to offer God praise and worship in community. Our identity, its meaning, and its theological implications can only unfold in the presence of God as God and we as God's creatures – "World remains world, God is God" yet we are in God. In this shape; the liturgy of God's Call; listening to God's Word; Going on the Journey with God; being sustained by Sacrament; and being sent into the world with a mission, we find our shape. The total shape of the book and the telling of God's great story of creation and redemption thus reflect the inherent sense of the argument that I am wishing to make. We find our shape in the shape of the worship of God. Christian spirituality is shaped in the context of the worship of God.

Formation in this book is used in the broad sense; it includes all people and their destiny in creation. For Christians this formation occurs in the context of the local Christian community and in the context of the journey. These two contexts are shaped by the big story, which shapes us. In as much as we need to understand anything of our faith, we need to understand how we fit into this story, how our community is called within it, and how together, we journey for God's reign. This is the arch criterion of the story.

Over the last thirty years I have served in active Christian ministry. Of this time, about five years was spent teaching part-time in a theological education setting, the last ten years that teaching ministry became full-time at a theological College, Knox College in Toronto where I presently serve as Professor of Systematic Theology. In this capacity I am passionately interested in what I am called to do and what we are called to do as those who walk with others on their journey of discovery, growth and sending into active leadership. The reflection on formation in this book is for all Christians being formed in local Christian communities and of course for all interested readers but it certainly applies very specifically also to what we do in a seminary context.

This book is about the big story of God and God's creation with view to what it means for us as community. In this sense it is also a book that tries to work out what spirituality means in our day and age and context. Spirituality has become a truly elusive term. It is particularly the vagueness of its popular use that makes it problematic. Moreover, this word often implies that it is about that which is disembodied, ethereal, and on the level of intuition and experience. I believe that limiting our understanding to these particular assumptions attached to the word spirituality may obscure the profound meaning of the word Spirit and spirit as it unfolds in the Hebrew and Greek texts of Scripture. A Judaeo-Christian vision of spirituality is rooted in the big story of God and God's creation. In this story the Spirit, Breath or Wind (Hebrew *Ruah)* of God hovers over the dark chaotic void and orders matter into being. This Spirit animates life and thus sustains creation on its most basic level. Such Spirit and the human spirit are thus always undeniably embodied. The Christian journey and the way God calls us into being is embodied and thus our spirituality is only true where it embodies our place in the big story. Matter matters.

If matter matters our experience is not to be separated from our bodily existence. We experience, feel, think and intuit in our bodies. Every example of these experiences and different forms of awareness can be related to our physical being in the world. In this sense neuro-scientific research that claims a link between weak magnetic fields and religious experience, such as Dr. Persinger's "god helmet"[4], would not refute the spiritual but would rather support the understanding that our created state enables our physiology to work with our process of experience, awareness, and finally our ability to make meaning out of it. Our embodied nature as creatures thus does not bring a competition between whatever science may discover and faith, but rather our embodied state makes sense of this in the light of the great narrative of God and creation. It is not in the discoveries of science, but rather in the ethics of scientific research and the assumptions of its power that there ought to be a debate between theology and science.

If matter matters then Christian spirituality is not just embodied, but like all matter in creation it is constantly being formed, it is on a journey, it is being shaped and it has a pilgrim character. We will explore the implications of eschatology, future promise and fulfillment in relation to this journey as we go along. Christian spirituality is thus about being, but it is not a static or passive being, it is being on a journey. Thus, David Bosch captured this well when he described Christian spirituality as a spirituality of the road. The Good Samaritan that stops to care for and love God's beaten up creature is walking a dusty road and is a pilgrim that demonstrates such conceptions of spirituality. As meditative and as prayerful as we must be, these dimensions can never be divorced from the pilgrim journey. We are called into being as human bodies in creation. This call dictates that we should live bodily in this reality.

This spirituality, formation on the journey, the response to the Call of God in worship is to be lived in the embodied reality of the world and in history. We can therefore not escape our own day and age – our context. Neither should we! This book will not remake an earlier argument I made about the technological and digital world we live in and its impact on our consciousness[5]. However, we will see that our theological reflection on God's great story and its implications for our formation as people, leaders and our spirituality is impacted by our present context in very particular ways. Christian formation is an ancient tradition and the institutions of this tradition presently face the challenge of radical and unrelenting change. The only thing that will probably not change is the reality of change itself!

I make no apology for advocating a big story in our so-called post-modern world. Some think of such claims of big stories that make sense of the world as coercive and therefore a power-grab in a world with many stories and explanations and many religious claims vying for power. I am sympathetic to the concern over coercion. If anything should become clear from our exploration of God's story in worship it is that God does not coerce creation. Freedom is the state for which creation is created. However, I believe that we need to be able to tell the story to enable us to be and act responsibly. We need to tell, to bear witness, and we need to walk the way. At the same time we need to do so with humility and without coercion.

Giving up on one's conviction of a truth claim for one's story basically removes one's premise for one's meaning as a person. Of course we know in part and we tell the story only with a limited, humble, and even vulnerable human state of limitation. Yet, such bold humility is most certainly required. Such humility knows enough to make sense, to live appropriately and with enough conviction to meet the challenge of life's journey and to shoulder the tasks before it while at the same time living with a profound sense of wonder of all it does not know and cannot explain.

Is the claim that there is no great story or final story not in itself a truth claim of sorts? Does it not coerce in its own way? There is a lot to be said for Leslie Newbigin insistence, after so many years of respectful dialogue among different religions in India, that the Christian faith does make truth claims. We do claim a final story albeit in a humble way, acknowledging our own limitations, our own possible misunderstandings, and our own dependence on God as we tell it. Yet tell it we must and tell it we shall. We are, as the Hindu proverb goes, beggars telling other beggars where to find food, but we are beggars that will not be quiet in the excitement of our discovery.

Preludes must not be too long. The worship shall now begin with poetry, stories and theological reflection. First, in Chapter One we will hear the Call to Worship, explore the meaning of Call and the evocation of the world and human beings by God. In Chapter Two, as with any gathering for worship, we will listen; we will listen to the Scriptures and listen for the call to repentance. In Chapter Three, we will contemplate the journey that our listening implies. In Chapter Four, we will see and taste the sacramental intention of God. In Chapter Five, we will be sent. Finally, we will enjoy the postlude as we prepare to go.

Now, as Johann Sebastian Bach put it musically, *Wachtet auf, ruft uns die Stimme*, Wake up, calls the voices to us! Or in the words of the Epistle writer, "Wake up, sleeper, and rise from death, and Christ will shine on you."

Notes

1. Swimme, Brian *The Universe Story: From the Primordial Flaring Forth to the Ecozoic Era: A Celebration of the Unfolding of the Cosmos.* New York: Harper Collins, 1994.

2. McCormack, Bruce L. *Karl Barth's Critically Realistic Dialectical Theology: Its Genesis and Development 1909-1936* Oxford: Clarendon Press, 1995, 21.

3. http://www.wired.com/wiredscience/2009/05/ribonucleotides/ (Accessed August 9, 2010).

4. http://en.wikipedia.org/wiki/Michael_Persinger (Accessed August 10, 2010).

5. Fensham, Charles J. *Emerging from the Dark Age Ahead: The Future of the North American Church.* Toronto: Clements Academic, 2011.

1

The Call

*Today if you shall hear his voice, harden
not your hearts.*

–(Hebrews 4:7, NASB)

The Call to Worship – The Greeting of Peace

The words kept echoing through my mind. I had no peace and no rest.
Driven by an obsessive thought process, I circled confused, yet aimless-
ly around the house. "Today if ye shall hear his voice, harden not your
hearts." These words drew me into the biblical story. It came from the
Book of Hebrews, it spoke to people long ago, yet strangely and goading-
ly, it seemed to speak to me. It was high summer, yet the lush growth in
the garden, the bright sunshine, and the delicious scent of Jasmine waft-
ing through the summer morning were lost on me. "Do not harden your
heart", these words would not go away. I had finished my second year in
Architecture School. I loved the creativity, the challenge of making new
things, and hanging out with my friends. I loved the rebellion against
the apartheid system of my home country. I loved that our school could
show up the system by hiding a black student in a niftily designed space in
the ceiling of the Architecture building. I loved Frank Lloyd Wright, Le
Corbusier, and Alvar Aalto – I wanted to be an architect. "Today, if you
hear my voice do not harden your hearts." My adolescent brain could not
process these words, neither could it shake them off. I had just returned
from being a leader at the Christian Summer camp, and now this!

My dad's home office door was open, and as he sat puffing his pipe
perched over the original text of the book of Job. He was translating but
not unaware of his son's strange behaviour. On my next pass a voice came
from inside, "boeta!" This was his term of endearment for me. "Boeta,
what is wrong?" "Wrong?" I breathed in youthful defiance – "nothing."

7

He had risen from behind his desk – he was not a man easily moved when at work. The question hung in the air, his disbelief palpable.

I found myself standing in front of his desk; he sat down and gestured to the easy chair behind me. He waited. He was a man who knew when to be quiet. I flopped down in the chair. "Well, pa, you see I was reading the Book of Hebrews this morning." He lifted his eyebrows; he was no small expert on this book having written a commentary on it..." Here's the thing, 'today if you hear my voice do not harden your hearts.'" He puffed on his pipe and kept quiet. "Well, I can't get these words out of my mind." "Ah", he said thoughtfully, "Perhaps God is calling you?" He had named the elephant in the room. I knew what it meant, at least I thought I did, and I did not like it. Strangely, as soon as I sighed the word, "yes" my sense of discomfort faded. A great burden was lifted.

To be called is to have a vocation. It gives meaning to one's life. We will see later that the story of creation itself is a story of evocation – a calling into being by God. This calling and creative narrative lies at the heart of all that I will explore in this book. But first we turn to the particularity of call in people's lives as we encounter it through biblical and Christian history.

Stories of call to leadership lie at the heart of the history of Christian formation for spirituality. One of the most important things we need to realise about such stories of call similar to the one told above is that they are highly personal and particular. As we will see later, particularity of call is one of the hallmarks of biblical stories of call. These stories are not to be read as models for the call of others, but rather to underline the message that God calls individuals in unique and particular ways. Such stories, although particular and contextual, always carry universal implications in the great unfolding story of creation and redemption. It is exactly the difference among call stories in the Bible that reinforces the awareness that different people will experience their particular call in life uniquely.

The very mention of experience in the context of call raises an important point. Even though it is undeniable that many biblical stories of call had dramatic elements of human experience in them, for example the call of Isaiah in a vision (Is 6) or Paul being struck to the ground and blinded (Acts 9:4), Moses at the burning bush (Ex. 3), or Abraham who "hears" or discerns God's call to move to a new land (Gen.12), experience remains a problematic measure of call. For Martin Luther his experience of peace and acceptance after striving so much to please God was a critical issue that led him to emphasise certainty in faith as a kind of experience. However, mystical or inner religious experience remains highly particular to the person who experiences it. John Calvin insisted that one should not look at yourself but rather at Christ for faith assurance. He was aware how inner experience can be doubtful and fickle. Calvin even accepted that doubt was a kind of flipside of faith in our human experience and understood that fickle feelings of certainty or doubt offer very little comfort on the faith journey. His was an attempt to turn the Christian journey away from self-absorption towards community discernment. Still today we can become obsessed with our experience rather than with the meaning of our existence based in God's creative purpose with creation.

By the 17th century the pietist movement in Germany and the Puritan movement started to emphasise experience more specifically and experience became fundamentally associated with certain religious feelings in the person. This new emphasis on experience and feeling probably arose out of the empiricist philosophy of the time that stressed appeal to experience as a way to prove something.[1] Such stress on experience had a huge impact on North American spirituality through Jonathan Edwards in the United States and later revival and camp meetings followed by the Pentecostal movement. John Wesley and the global Methodist movement also stand in this tradition that emphasises religious experience. The 19th century German theologian, Friedrich Schleiermacher, considered the architect of modern liberal theology, described faith as "gefühl", a word that indicated the full range of human experience as well as feeling.

Religious experience of this kind tended to individualise faith and the call to follow God as it merged with the theory of the autonomous individual that arose out of the Enlightenment movement in Europe. Whether we like it or not, we live in a cultural milieu where personal experience and particularly individualised experience and feeling has become a basic assumption of our cultural world. We only need to listen to ourselves when we make an argument, how often do we say, "I feel that…."?

It is clear that a sense of call and direction in one's life as a person and the meaning that arises from faith that God calls one in a direction is very important and has always been a key element of biblical stories of call. It is also clear that an excessive emphasis on experience, particularly extraordinary individual experience, can be frustrating and painful to those who never seem to experience such particular feelings. Moreover, those who do claim special experiences and feelings may in some cases consider themselves spiritually elevated above those who don't. Mixed with individualism such religious experience can lead to isolation or cult-like spirituality that depends on insights and feelings of particularly "gifted" individuals. Despite these cautions we also need to recognise that we cannot access or engage life, others, stories, art, religious texts and so on without experience. When we speak of experience in this way we are speaking not of it in narrow individual feeling only, but more so in the sense of being, feeling, hearing, responding, sensing in our context and culture. Today we recognise that culture also constructs our experience. These constructions can be both positive and negative for human beings as they live together. Our religious texts can also cause destructive constructions such as the way the Apartheid regime in South Africa constructed narratives of racism out of biblical texts in the Old Testament, or they way women or people of minorities could be constructed by culture to be excluded, judged and harmed[2].

In response to the exploration of experience and call above we need to observe that call cannot be divorced from experience nor from the feelings that we have as individuals. Call can also not be reduced to experience and feelings of the individual and needs more substance behind it. Traditionally Christian churches have emphasised the role of community in connection with call. It is the community together who discern call and leadership. Whether the individual has a "liver shivering" experience or not does not determine call. In fact, as we will see later St. Augustine was so resistant to the idea of a call to become bishop that he did not go anywhere where there was need of a bishop! He was forced to be ordained by a congregation rather than coming forward and offering himself. Consistently, in all the biblical stories of call, God's call was a call to community. I will suggest below that the way the journey of the individual, including their experience, is integrated with the role and place of community is through story. All biblical examples of call are examples of the community of faith telling stories of the call of their leaders. For Christian spirituality in our own time, we need to recover the communal telling of our stories of call as we build meaning and identity.

Resistance

Curiously, in the history of the church, resistance of call or reticence to take it up makes up a common theme. Such resistance is particularly notable among the male leaders of the early Christian movement. Even though we cannot find a strong sense of resistance of call in the stories of the first disciples as recorded in the Gospels, resistance seemed to become common in early Christian male piety. Perhaps this early piety is in imitation of Moses' call at the burning bush or the call of the prophets Isaiah and Jeremiah? Perhaps it can even be traced to the ironic resistance of the prophet Jonah? Resistance was also linked to a developing other-worldly spirituality that started valuing individual withdrawal and ascetic piety over the community of faith and its embodied living in the world. Thus the desert monastics in their individual piety and rigorous self-denial became a kind of ideal as opposed to the distractions and messiness of dealing with the local Christian community, its conflicts and machinations.

We find this pattern of reticence in the life of Gregory of Nazianzus (330-389) when he was invited to take up duties as bishop. After his coercive ordination in 361 he fled. When he returned he complained about his diocese, "How slow you are my friends, and brethren to listen to my words, though you are so swift in tyrannizing over me and tearing me from my Citadel Solitude."[3] Longing for solitude and meditation he resisted his appointment as bishop of Constantinople and ascribed his final acquiescence as due, not to his own will, but by the coercion of others.[4] Despite being under constant threat and having to suffer much opposition, Gregory would give the church one of its most precious gifts – insight into the divinity of the Holy Spirit.

John Chrysostom's (347-407) life tells a similar tale. He was an unimposing man whose health was weak due to injudicious asceticism. In appearance he was not much of an oil painting either! One author describes him as having a large bald head with a lofty wrinkled forehead, deep-set piercing eyes, and a prominent nose with a wispy beard.[5] A description that makes most of us feel a little bit better about ourselves... John had a crafty side and made a pact with his friend Basil to be ordained bishops without ever intending to fulfil his end of the bargain. Basil, thus tricked into a bishopric, was less than impressed. In John's *Six Books on the Priesthood* he recounts his resistance against being ordained a priest. It is not clear if these stories are used to reinforce the seriousness of vows or actually represented biographical material. However, John does continue to reinforce the tradition that seemed to contrast the call to community leadership as priest or bishop against the call to a life of withdrawal, prayer and asceticism. John eventually became known as the man with the golden tongue due to his powerful preaching. Reticence to be ordained is also recorded about Pope Gregory the Great (540-604), who resisted both his ordination as deacon and later his appointment as Pope.

The great architect of Western Theology, Saint Augustine (354-430), dramatically illustrates the reticence of call to Christian leadership both in his ordination as priest and later as bishop. His ordination as priest occurred in the North African city of Hippo when he went there to support a friend who was on a spiritual quest. After a sermon by Bishop Valerius that outlined the need for Christian leaders, the congregation turned on Augustine and forced him to the altar to be ordained.[6] About ordination to bishop Augustine wrote, "I feared the office of bishop to such an extent that, as soon as my reputation came to matter among 'servants of God', I would not go to any place where I knew there was no bishop."[7]

Women committed to call

Due to the way patriarchal culture constructed early Christian stories we do not have that many stories of the spiritual journeys of women. However, some important traditions survive.

> "While we were under arrest, my father out lf love for me was trying to persuade me and shake my resolution. "Father," said I, "do you see this vase here, for example, or waterpot or whatever?" "Yes, I do," said he. And I told him, "Could it be called by any other name than what it is?" And he said, "No." "Well, so too I cannot be called anything other than what I am, a Christian." (From the martyrdom of Perpetua)[8]

Thus Perpetua (181-203), a woman of 22 years old replied when her family tried to sway her from her call to bear witness to Christ. In fact, in the ancient story of her martyrdom she turns out to be leader among a group of men and women on their way to their death in the Roman arena. Here there is no whiff of resistance of call or shirking responsibility in the small community in prison with other catechumenate among whom Perpetua found herself. Even though stories of early Christian martyrs are often considered suspect by historians because of their tendency to exaggerate the perfection of saints, it is clear that this was an inspirational story of a woman's commitment and leadership as a Christian that functioned as encouragement to many Christians.

Another good example of a woman eager to serve God and the community of faith is the sister of Bishop Gregory of Nyssa, Macrina. Not only did Macrina long to serve God in prayer and monastic life, she also inspired her mother to voluntarily dispense with the social hierarchy between servants and mistress and to share all within her household equally.[9] Thus Macrina becomes an example, admired by her brother the famous bishop for her leadership in faith and her challenge for unjust social practices.

Clearly, women responded to God's call in these early days in committed and exemplary ways. It is perhaps harder to judge if these stories should be compared in contrast to the male resistance described above. Part of our problem is that the role of women in the honour-shame Greco-Roman culture of the time never gave them the opportunity to turn down bishoprics! Nevertheless, within their context these women set an inspiring example. We may ask ourselves if we would be as faithful as Perpetua in the face of death, or if we would be as courageous as Macrina's mother in challenging the oppressive economic and political structures of her time? However, we must note that our own time is filled with people who have lived their faith courageously. We can think of Dietrich Bonhoeffer during the Second World War who paid with his life for resistance against Hitler. I think personally of Rosina Mpalele, a Presbyterian elder in South Africa who was imprisoned without trial for trying to make peace. We can think also Edith Stein, Sister Dorothy Kazel, Martin Luther King, Bishop Desmond Tutu and many more seldom mentioned faithful ones. Such courageous faith is perhaps not so much our doing as the special gift of grace given by God when it is required...

Call Today

During early times Christian vocation involved a sense of risk and commitment; it was a choice people made in the face of many challenges. Through the history of the Christian faith, concepts of vocation have gone through many changes. In medieval times vocation was considered something connected with a special monastic or church commitment. Of course such exemplary practice still continues today. During the reformation, vocation or calling became a concept that included the idea that one's daily work could be part of vocation. For much of the modern period this protestant idea of vocation played a formative role in shaping people's sense of meaning in life. In our Post-Christian context significant questions are being raised about vocation. Thus William Placher writes,

> The very claim that there is something that God wants me to do with my life, for instance, threatens many contemporary definitions of freedom. Surely, I can do whatever I want with my life, and the choice is mine? Much of the Christian tradition, however, has argued that that vision of life as a sea of infinite choices is more like slavery than freedom.[10]

In sympathy with Placher's argument I would suggest that the seemingly limitless and expanding world of choice and information andconstant technological change requires a new emphasis on God's call and vocation within the world of Christian faith. If we are to think seriously about formation for Christian spirituality, then surely, a renewed focus and a deepened and contextually shaped understanding of Christian vocation for women and men is necessary.

So far we have been concerned with the experience of call and vocation in terms of some historical figures. This historical perspective on traditions of vocation is very important because it provides models and metaphors for our reflection on call and formation in this book. However, my pivotal argument in this book is that we need to understand call, vocation, and formation for

Christian spirituality in terms of the narrative of God's creative and redemptive work. In this the opening chapters of the Book of Genesis provides us with all we need. What follows is an invitation to the reader to explore ways of reading the opening chapters of the Book of Genesis that will seek to honour the formation of these ancient texts and their final form during the period of Israel's exile, while seriously conversing with vocation in our time and place. Calling, I argue, is not just something that happens to us as human beings for a vocation during our lifetimes, more importantly, calling is integrated with the way of God's creation. The very act of creation is an act of God calling forth. The "Word" that becomes such an important concept in Christian theology, has its genesis in God's gracious act of creation. All things are constituted by God's call and out of such deep and profound loving call proceeds our call as human beings. To get formation for Christian spirituality right we need to grasp this profound connection between God's creating Word that calls forth creation and God's gracious word that brings redemption.

Called into Being: The Evocative God in Biblical Narratives

In his introduction to his commentary on the Book of Genesis the American author and Old Testament scholar Walter Breuggemann[11] argues that the Book of Genesis is basically a book of call. There are two movements to the calling action of God. First God calls forth the world to be God's faithful world. This theme is covered in Genesis 1-11. Secondly God's calls specific people to be God's faithful people. The calling of particular people and their response is covered in Genesis 12-50.[12] Thus, both creation **and** the community of faith are "evoked by the speech of this God."[13] God is thus described and revealed to us as a calling God in the opening book of the Bible. This means that God is known in creation through God's calling Word that goes forth and creates. This creation is not simply something made beside and beyond God, but God's calling presence evokes and invites response from creation – creation stands in relationship with God. Creation is called and we are called. In particular we are called to respond to God. Both creation and humankind thus find their identity, according to the narratives of Genesis, in vocation. To be human is to be called forth by God and then to be called by God for a special task in creation. This is who we are. Christian spirituality starts here.

God calls us, and, at the same time, that call comes to us from God in the shape of a promise. Promise means that God calls creation and humankind forward on a journey in and towards the promise. Not only does God call and expect response, God also promises engagement and a future. We can characterise this creating, calling, and responding process as the root of the Mission of

God often described in 20th century ecumenical literature as the *Missio Dei* (the Latin for Mission of God). Creation and people are called forth and then called to a task with a future. In theology this movement of calling towards and moving forwards to a goal is described by the word eschatology. Eschatology and mission, to be called with a promise and sent, is thus embedded in the unfolding of the Scriptural story. We can thus say that Breuggemann teaches us that the Book of Genesis is at its heart a book of mission.[14]

The Book of Genesis outlines God's process of call in four dimensions. These are God's "sovereign call" (Genesis 1-11:29),"the embraced call of God" (Genesis 11:30-25:18-the story of Abraham as the father of faith and the blessing to all nations), "the conflicted call of God" (Genesis 25:19-36:43-the story of Jacob) and finally, "the hidden call of God" (Genesis 37-50:62-the story of Joseph).[15] In recounting these different stories of call, the Book of Genesis captures the core issues in the experience of call from the human perspective. It also illustrates the whole journey of faith as a journey of call and promise.

In addition to these four dimensions of call in Genesis, we can also detect two dimension of call in the first three chapters of Genesis. We can identify these as the "creative call of God" and the "agonising call of God". The first is obvious, all of creation is called forth in the face of chaos and the dark void or deep waters by God's creative word. The second call – the agonising call of God – is less obvious, but illustrates the difference between the Hebrew concept of the God who created the universe as opposed to the views of the surrounding nations.[16] Against the fickle Sumerian or Babylonian gods the Hebrew exiles confessed and proclaimed a God that stood in a fundamentally different relation to God's creation. God's sovereignty is expressed not in capricious use of absolute power, but, in the words of Breuggemann, "Sovereign power as faithfulness, patience and anguish."[17] He continues, "We are dealing here with a peculiar kind of sovereignty. This sovereign speech is not coercive but evocative. Thus it may be resisted and unheeded. But the call of the creator is not thereby voided."[18] The real potential inherent in creation for creatures to resist God and not to heed God's call is soon realised in the unfolding story of the first three chapters of Genesis. Human rebellion leads to the second kind of call, the call of anguish, the one we discover in Genesis 3:9, when God calls out to the human creatures in what is rendered in the Hebrew language in one agonising word, "Where?" (*A'hee*).

When I read Genesis 3:9, I cannot help but remember when I lost my toddler son in a large department store. In an unguarded moment he wandered away and the agony and searing fear that passed through me as I frantically called "Andrew!" is stuck in my memory. The great Divine sigh of agony captured in Genesis 3:9 can be imagined as such a parental call. It is the call of the faithful and patient One who would not let humankind go and hide. This is not a God who is untouched by our fate. This is not the God of Greek philosophy that is so beyond creation that its rebellion and suffering is not shared. This is an impassioned God. Reading this text in this way suggests that the suffering of a broken relationship is first experienced within God before it becomes apparent to the creatures foolishly hiding. God shares the suffering of the broken bond and loss of faithfulness to the covenantal relationship of love and responsibility. The freedom of God's creatures to obey or to rebel does not only bring the potential that God may suffer, the potential is realised. Whereas the calling forth of creation by the creative Word is an act that cannot be resisted, the calling of humankind and creation to its covenantal journey of promise and faithfulness can be resisted. According to this story we can resist and we do. Now the sovereign, faithful, and patient God is in anguish in relation to God's cherished and beautiful creation. We can observe that this way of reading and understanding this text underlines God's fundamental solidarity with the rebellious human and with the devastating destructive impact of human rebellion on creation. God does not turn God's back on the rebellious human. God does not cancel this creation to start a new one. God, who loves and cherishes creation like a child will not let it go wrong. In this sense God is already in this early text in solidarity with the "poor" if part of what it is to be poor is to be alienated from God. To be "Godless" is thus to suffer marginalisation, struggle, violence, and pain because of such alienation. The cowering humans foolishly hiding are the poor in spirit but do not realise it until they hear God's call, "Where?"

As humankind we stand before this dual call. We are called forth as creatures of the good and cherished creation and we are called forth in anguish as we run and hide in the garden. That this insight brought comfort during the exile in Babylon, when despair and alienation wracked the people of faith, makes it more powerful and real for all of us who face our own alienations and our own rebellions. The fact that these texts gained currency during the Babylonian exile help us to see in a more graphic way just how important these texts are for our own self-understanding, and for our understanding of godlessness and alienation, suffering and poverty in our own time. Like they spoke to the Hebrew exiles to lift them up and establish identity and hope as slaves in the midst of a foreign land, these texts tell us who we are in the "foreign lands" of consumer and technological culture or global empires of finance that exploit and destroy creation and people. It is here that we need to start if we want to talk about Christian spirituality. The message of call – God's call that raises up and affirms human vocation, purpose, and meaning in the midst of creation –

provides us with profound identity. The message of God's agonizing call in the face of our resistance calls us to repentance and provides hope. Together people and creation stand under God's dual call which sets them free. It is to have God call after us and then to cover our shame with clothes fashioned from the earth. To have God promise that it will be made right again is to know that we are truly children of the faithful one. We are this – God's children – and not even our rebellion can undo this. In fact as lost children we are no less children.

So, creation is broken and we want to keep breaking it yet God calls and promises. This is the state of affairs to which we respond when we see the truth of this story. It is in this story and through this story that we can live as Christians. Christian spirituality and Christian leadership as well as the formation of our spiritual lives start here. The creative call of God speaks of the life-giving and liberating power of God's solidarity with humankind and creation. The anguished call of God speaks of the call to human repentance in God's redemptive purpose. Creation is not abandoned but the great promise resounds, "I will bring all things together in reconciliation!" In a dramatic way this basic Genesis narrative outlines a key theme that will play out in the great story of redemption through Abraham and his family in Jesus Christ. It is of prime importance that the central metaphor of the relationship of God and creation is not a philosophical abstraction, but rather, relationship.

So if this is what it is all about, why this thing that is called the church? What does it have to do with spirituality? It is so imperfect would we not be better off dumping it and pursuing being "spiritual" in some other more holy way?

Christian Spirituality is a Call to a Community at Work to Bring All Things Together

After the resurrection of Jesus the early Christians had to make sense of what Jesus meant and particularly who he was. The memories and sayings of Jesus and the of course the cross and the resurrection lead them by the year 325 to the surprising conclusion that God is a community of Father, Son and Spirit. For the early Hebrew Christians this was a very difficult idea. Everything taught in the faith of Abraham and Sarah and the prophets made this impossible. Every good Jew would confess the *Shema* "Hear O Israel the Lord your God is One." The early Christians certainly did not let go of this, they insisted that there is only one God – the God and Father of Jesus Christ. Yet this one God is also a community and intimate whole of three. The Gospel of John, the latest of the four Gospel have Jesus protesting over and over again, "I and the Father are one." In this way early Christians started to grasp for language to express the unity of

God and even fought over the way to say this right. One proposal which gained support over time was to understand the unity of God in terms of the deep inseparable love that binds Father, Son and Spirit together in mutual relationship. This means that the Trinity is one in unbroken ongoing unceasing and binding love that moves closely and intimately from Father to Son, From Son to Father, from Spirit to Father and Son that God is community in one communion of wholeness. The Lord your God is indeed One and yet community. The wise bishop, Gregory of Nazianzus, called this close relationship in oneness – *perichoresis* – in the Greek language. This word meant that God's unity is expressed in an unstoppable dynamic process of the Father giving himself to the Son, the Son giving himself to the Father and the Spirit giving herself to the Father and the Son and so on and on and on. If your head is reeling by reading all this you are not alone! We are trying to use the limited power of human words to describe God! But, imagine the love that binds you to the human person you love or loved most in your life. Imagine the closeness – unity if you wish – that such love achieved. Now imagine this kind of love intensified in Divine intensity! Such is the ongoing self giving love that makes God one yet a community of Father, Son, and Spirit. Creation and humankind are now invited to share in that love....

This is why God's creative call establishes humankind as community and not as autonomous and isolated individuals. This means that these early stories of Genesis challenge us to critique the very basis on which the whole of Western society and most of global society operates – the assumption of autonomous individualism. This is dramatically expressed in Genesis 1:27 when the sentence construction takes on a peculiar form. "So God created the human person in God's own image (singular), male and female God created them (plural)." Both Old Testament scholars Walter Breuggemann and John Sailhamer point out that the movement from the inclusive singular "God created the human person" to the defined plural, "male and female God created them", can be read as an explanation of what is meant by "in God's own image".[19] This idea was explored earlier by the famous twentieth century Swiss theologian Karl Barth. It is worth quoting Barth here,

> "Not only is God's image expressed in the ability to stand in personal relationship with God, but also in the ability to form a community of relationship as we find in the couple of man and woman." [20]

This means there is no image of God simply in an isolated individual. We need to reify this into gendered relationship, but rather, we could see how this metaphor of relationship points to a state of relationality as a profound and divine dimension of the human condition. This image of God always requires a community to reflect the community of God. The first thing Jesus did was call disciples to walk with him and form a community. And though we know today that this community included both men and women, it was not a relationality rooted in gender based exclusivity but rather an inclusive relationality of people loving each other. There is no Christian spirituality without community and community points to the church.

As the second creation story, which is probably older than Genesis 1, is told in Genesis 2, community again becomes a critical dimension of the story. The creation of the female completes what it is to be human and this completeness in community requires a whole separate creation initiative from God. Nothing but the woman as another human being will do to make human community, not plants, trees, birds, animals or even the Divine companion. If we read these stories through this lens, humans are called forth from the dark void and destined to be human only in community. Every human individual needs an "other" to be truly human. A fundamental part of vocation is the call to community, a call to be with and for the other.

To be called forth by the creative word of God is to be called to community. What is lost by the humans in the unfolding story of Genesis 3 is exactly community. The man and woman hide, they blame each other and community and communion is broken. In a mirror-like way, the agonising call of God in the garden – "Where?"- responds to this broken community. These observations from the opening chapters of the Bible establish the dual call of humankind to community and return to community as our identity as people. Christian spirituality and Christian leadership always progress from these two basic constitutive calls. To be called as an individual is always a call to and in community. This community can take many forms all rooted in the deep love that we as people are able to share with one another. The form and experience of a particular call will vary greatly among different people, yet it is God that calls, the God that called forth creation, and the God that called after Adam and Eve in the garden. This is what we call Good News or evangelism. To evangelise is to tell this Good News and invite others to community with one another and God. Where there is true loving human community whatever its constituent part there God is never far away.

Christian Spirituality is Rooted in Stories

> Telling stories is as basic to human beings as eating. More so, in fact,
> for while food makes us live, stories are what make our lives worth
> living. They are what make our condition *human.*[21]

Any individual call is biographical. Such a call gains it's meaning in relation to
telling the story of call in community. We find our identity in the way we are
able to tell the stories of our lives. They are, as the quote from the Irish Christian philosopher Richard Kearney above suggests," ...what makes life worth living". The question is not if the story is dramatic, or earth shaking, or mundane,
rather, the question is – does it make my life worth living? We can also phrase
it differently, "is it life-giving and liberating from broken relationship and injustice?" For the person of faith the question becomes, "how does my story fit
in the bigger narrative that constitutes my faith? How does my story fit with
God's creative call that brings me into being? How does my story work with
God's call to me for a vocation in community in freedom and limitation?" Perhaps this would be a good time to ask yourself these questions as you read...

Our identities as people are narrative identities. Narratives are not created
to be individually hidden but to be shared. After all, what is the point of a story
if you cannot share it with someone else? This is why pastoral care and pastoral
healing is deeply intertwined with how we are able to tell the story of our lives.
The healing process is aided as we re-tell our stories in the faith community as
we make sense of senseless, painful, and alienating life experiences.[22] Each person has some kind of story of call. For some it might be abrupt and overt like the
story told at the beginning of this chapter, for others it might be an unfolding
story of sensing direction in life. Dag Hammarskjöld, former Secretary General
of The United Nations, described his call thus,

> "I don't know Who–or what–put the question... But at some mo-
> ment I did answer Yes to Someone–or Something–and from that
> hour I was certain that existence is meaningful and that, therefore,
> my life, in self-surrender, had a goal."[23]

Stories make us human in the theological spiritual sense of the word. It human-
ises the seeming meaningless march of experiences and events in our lives that
we know as time.[24] Through the telling of our stories, our lives gain a sense
of coherence.[25] When such stories are told and re-told in community they establish our identity as individuals and community together. Thus stories create
meaning and communion. To live spiritually as Christians means to be able to

tell our own individual stories in a community and to understand them in the light of the stories of Genesis.

It is therefore important for our understanding of spirituality to realise that the narratives of Genesis are communicative acts. By calling them communicative acts we mean that these stories imply an audience; they are Good News or Gospel or preaching in the purest sense of these words. Even as these stories, compiled by wise Hebrews, are communicative acts in themselves, they describe the very act of creation as a communicative event. Genesis 1 is a great liturgical poem, which employs the refrain amar elohim "Said God" or "God said…" at the beginning of each day of creation. The "audience" of God's communicative act of creation is the dark void, chaos and the formless deep waters which responds to this communicative act as it is shaped into light, the world and so on. It is likely that the opening sentence of Genesis 1, "In the beginning God created the heavens and the earth" is to be understood as creation out of nothing (creatio ex nihilo in Latin). Whether we assume a creatio ex nihilo or not-and the text seems to leave both options open-creation itself is a communicative event and God is a communicative God[26]. The "Word of God" is never just a single word; it is a communication string implying God as speaker together with a community of hearers and responders. The Word of God therefore implies communion and community. From a human point of view we learn the identity of God through these stories of God, and in them we find our own identity. We learn that we are addressed and in being addressed and thus we find meaning and purpose.

If we follow the argument above it means that our universal calls and our calls as individuals-our vocation-is essentially a matter of imitation: it is, to use a popular term these days, mimetic. The word mimesis is usually simply understood to mean imitation, however, as Richard Kearney points out, for the Greek philosopher Aristotle this concept meant much more than simple imitation. "When Aristotle defines *mimesis* in his *Poetics* as the 'imitation of an action', he means a creative re-description of the world such that hidden patterns and hitherto unexplored meanings can unfold."[27] In our living out of the story of creation we re-describe the world to reveal its meaning. [28] We can say we demonstrate meaning and we always do it as community together, never just as isolated and autonomous individuals. By living we demonstrate the meaning of creation.

We can see from the earlier exploration of the Book of Genesis, that the centrality of story for meaning and the creative Word essentially made a similar case for the lost and alienated Hebrews in Babylon. Our stories of call retrieve the ancient narrative and fit us into it so as to make time meaningful and give life purpose. Our individual stories of call will have a uniqueness and particularity to it that is not shared by anyone, yet they will also have a meaning making *mimetic* or imitative dimension that will relate them to the great unfolding story of call and mission in the Scriptures.

In this process of storied purpose making the basic structure of call and promise in the Genesis narratives is brought to our attention. Having a promise that makes the direction of our lives clear, we are living towards an end, and for people of faith this does not simply mean a pipe dream, but a real hope that makes life worth living. This means that vocation and stories of vocation are what gives meaning to our lives and direct our lives to the future in hope. This also means that the structure of these biblical stories imply that we are created as human beings to thrive when we live in the tension between the stories that make sense of our world and that express our calling in this world and the hope in God's promises that draw us forward to live meaningful lives. In the long Christian tradition we have called this structure of living in the present with hope for the future the eschatological nature of our Christian journeys. The word *eschaton* ("end" in Greek) has been used to describe the last things or the end and purpose of creation. In the New Testament the story of Jesus becomes an eschatological event. This means that in the coming of Jesus some of the end or last things have already come while we are also waiting, hoping and working with the faith that the full promise will be realised. Vocation focuses communities and the individual on this purposeful end or fulfillment of God's promise. Living in vocation also focuses communities and individuals on already experiencing a part of what is to come at the end. The eschatological nature of vocation is a critical element of spirituality that should fundamentally shape our understanding of formation for vocation. Thus stories of call that we share in community do not only tie us back to our meaning and origin, but they also tie us forward to God's call, purpose and mission.

In the Western world it is extremely important to remember that community is essential to Christian spirituality. We come from a culture that has been shaped by a constant drive towards individualism. Yet, the stories we explored here that tell us who we are and how we function as human creatures consistently challenges us to bring our beautiful created individuality to community and to live in a community of vocation where our individuality – that which makes us unique and special – contributes to the whole community of creation and people. In fact we can argue that the structure of the story in Genesis 3 tells us that the beauty of individuality in the differences among Adam, Eve and God, is what is lost when individuality becomes individualism – Adam against Eve, Eve against Adam, Adam and Eve against God. Unfortunately, certain forms of Christian spirituality that developed in the 19th and 20th centuries have often missed this central truth. Spirituality which is understood as focused on *my* salvation, the benefits that I gain from faith, and my place in heaven, reflects Western culture's drive to selfish individualism rather than the call to a caring community with God's creation and creatures. Many of the old favourite hymns, despite great beauty and truth contained in them, often also fall victim to a kind of spiritual self-centeredness. In its most extreme forms this kind of spirituality claims a kind of individualistic personal relationship with God that directs the individual in isolation from the great stories in which our individual call rests. In contrast, the Genesis texts indeed call us to walk personally with God as unique individuals, but it is always a walk together with creation, people and God. It is never a walk focused on my benefit, rather it is a call focused on the wholeness (salvation) I share as I care for creation and work for the reconciliation of all people and things. Christian spirituality is indeed essentially about salvation. However, it is not an attenuated selfish "me and my God" salvation, it is a broad vision of the bringing together – reconciliation – of all things in God's wonderful creation. Jewish Rabbis who read the texts from Genesis speak of the *tikkun olam* – the task of world repair.[29]

On Liturgy and Doxology

You are called to tell the story, passing words of life along, then to blend your voice with others as you sing the sacred song[30].

This book is structured with reference to the early traditions of Christian worship. This is not accidental even though the outline of the book takes some liberties with this structure. The public service of the worship of God (liturgy) and the praise of God (doxology) are the ways that I choose to tell the story of God's call and formation to Christian spirituality. According to early accounts such as that of Justin Martyr (100-165), early Christian worship basically consisted of two parts, Word and Sacrament. This structure shapes public worship into a Divine-human conversation. The structure of the gathering of Christians in worship has traditionally been called "liturgy". The roots of this word go back to the idea of a public duty to worship God. According to the stories we have explored in Genesis so far, liturgy is represented as a communicative event and in this event God is always, without exception the subject. The human work of worship is always a response to God who calls. Liturgy in this sense always starts with God's agonising call to us "where?"

It is therefore no accident that the opening chapter of the Book of Genesis is a liturgy in its own right. This liturgy is both word, in the shape of call and promise, and sacrament, in the shape of a visible sign of God's grace. Later we will explore the idea of sacrament in a whole chapter of this book, for now, it is important to note the importance of sacrament. I believe that we find the sacramental dimension in the opening stories of the bible particularly where the creation of the humans is described as being in the image of God. If sacrament is the visible sign of God's invisible grace on earth[31], we can argue that there is a way in which humankind as community is sacramental as a sign of God's grace. Humankind becomes a visible representation of God's graciousness and love in the act of creation. Of course, this human representation, traditionally described as *Imago Dei* (Image of God) must not be taken too far. It is helpful to note here that at least some commentators who note that another translation for the word traditionally rendered as "image" is shadow[32]. The human community as *shadow images* of God places appropriate parameters around the profound claim of Genesis 1:26 that humankind in some way represents God. What we can say with conviction is that humankind has a sacramental purpose in creation. We are to be visible representations of God's graciousness to creation and one another. This makes the sacramental dimension in spirituality and Christian worship and essentially ecological task. The imagination to grasp this task is conveyed in the Judeo- Christian tradition through poetry.

The poetic and liturgical power of the first chapter of Genesis is so strong that it penetrates even the veil of translation. Within this biblical liturgy the story of God's creative acts are told, and in the telling, the relationship between God and creation finds it's meaning in call and promise. In the telling God is in conversation with the cherished and beloved creation and humankind are both part of this creaturely state and a task to be completed in representing God. Creation is evoked by the speech of God. Humankind's destiny is spoken forth. In this way God's creative call and our own individual stories of call are drawn into the liturgy and doxology of the coming together of all things in creation.

God remains the undeniable subject of the Genesis account. We have already noticed how the human being is defined in relation to God as being-in-community. We have hinted at the inverted and almost subversive description of God's sovereignty as exercised in faithfulness, patience and anguish. Call understood within the context of liturgy can never lose sight of God as subject. Human experience, human community, and human stories that make meaning of our lives and times all have their origin, their reality, their very existence rooted in God as subject. As I pointed out in the prelude the Book of Acts reports Paul appropriating the famous poem of the Greek poet Epimenides, "In

God we live and move and have our being" (Acts 17:28), which is an excellent expression of the primacy of God as subject in the liturgy of our call as human beings. We do not exist as humans versus God we exist as humans in God. The human response to such a subject in the Divine-human conversation is doxology or praise. This also means that as humans we concretize our praise to God in being in loving community with one another and the rest of creation as we tend and care for it as a community representing God. This means that caring for God's creation glorifies God and is a profound expression of doxology. This also means that a concern for ecology, in Christian spirituality is not simply a fad or a desperate attempt to save a dying biosphere; it is the fundamental element of the glorification of God as presented to us in the opening creation accounts of the Hebrew Scriptures.

In this way of thinking our lives and their meaning are constituted in vocation with God as subject. Even as the whole of creation is the subject of the Divine Liturgy of creation, so our lives fit into this liturgy and respond in doxology. Our response to God's missional call is in itself a form of doxology. Our joyous ecological responsibility is clear in this vocation of worship.

On Call as Promise

Breuggemann's analysis that points to the strong theme of promise in the Genesis narrative provides another vital dimension to this reflection on call and vocation to Christian spirituality. Breuggemann remarks,

> "*Promise* weaves in and out of the narrative. At times it is explicit and intrinsic to the texts. At other times, it is imposed on the text in a secondary way. At still other times it is only implicit and not stated at all. But in all three cases, primary, secondary, and implicit, the persistent claims is that God has promised to stay with his called partner until his way is accomplished. The partner-creation/Israel-is called to rely only on God's promise.[33]"

The Genesis narratives thus present us with an interwoven fabric of call and promise. In the face of the invasion of sin, God's call to individual people implies the promise of a future; the promise of redemption. Thus, call and promise have to do with the coming of God grace. God's grace continues to overwhelm whatever human actions go against God's purpose for creation. Sin, even though it lurks in every story, can never overcome God's grace. The irrepressibility of grace is the energy of call. Called ones fall into sin, fail, and turn the wrong way, yet God's grace continues on, calling and promising towards a future. These elements of grace become the promise of the coming reign of God, called "the Kingdom" in the New Testament. Thus we return again to our earlier assertion that call and vocation is an eschatological event. God's faithfulness despite the waywardness of the called ones in Genesis provided a powerful encouragement and hope to the exiles in Babylon as they pondered these stories by the rivers of Babylon. They experienced themselves as lost, yet they were able to imagine God's promise as still powerfully relevant to them.

God's call connects us with meaning, purpose and end. God's call announces destiny. It is easy, within a North American or Western context to individualise the idea of meaning, purpose and end. Destiny can easily be truncated to my individual destiny. This is not so with any of the Genesis narratives. Eve and Adam have inseparable destiny, the same with Cain and Abel, and, of course Noah does not go into the Ark alone. Abraham's call and destiny is wrapped up with the blessing of all nations, extending call to the broadest imaginable scope, and so on. Call towards the future promise, is always a call in relationship. In this the Genesis narrative is clear – God maintains the initiative. To put it in Breuggemann's words, "When the facts warrant death, God insists on life for his creatures."[34]

Call as eschatological event also contains part of the promise in the present reality. God graciously clothes Adam and Eve after the Fall to hide their own embarrassment. God's gracious covering thus already realises part of what is to come – full reconciliation – in the now. Even though Abraham would become the father of many nations in promise, he only becomes father to one son in his present reality, and so we can continue to see the pattern of grace already given and grace unrealised in experience and only anticipated in the future.

On Call and Blessing

The original call of creation is a call to blessing. Perhaps the most dramatic way this is illustrated in the Genesis narrative is in God's cherishment of creation on the seventh day. Intrinsic to creation itself is the Sabbath – the blessing and cherishing of the beauty and rightness of creation. In fact, there is a sense in which the cherishment of creation in the creation accounts relays a sense of aesthetic cherishment. It is not so much "good" in the ethical sense of the word, as beautiful or pleasing[35]. God's life-giving work intrinsic to creation is what constitutes the original concept of blessing. Blessing then has to do with the vital link between God and creation that is there despite a qualitative distinction between God and creation that the Hebrews emphasised. The blessing and cherishment of creation means that God will neither abandon creation nor will God withdraw the freedom within limits given to creation[36].

Call, Fear and Mastery

"...and I was afraid..." (Adam to God in the Garden, Genesis 3:10, NASB)

The wholesome cherished creative call of humankind to communion in community is radically altered in the garden when God's agonising cry "where?" evokes fear. The first human response to alienation is to master it by means of technology–"and they sowed fig leaves together and made themselves aprons"– the second is fear followed shortly afterwards by blaming. Breuggemann shows that this process finds its end in a move from freedom in vocation to a focus the isolated individual as "I". The narrative underlines it with the sudden intrusion of "I"; "I heard. I was afraid. I was naked.[37]" The rupture of community is dramatic and revealing. God's agonised call seeking communion with the human contains judgement and promise, severity and grace.

It is therefore not surprising that the individual call to Christian leadership has often evoked reticence in the one called. In a sense this reticence represents the most basic temptation of Christian spirituality. Gregory of Nazianzus' complaint about being drawn back into community, that we mentioned earlier, illustrates how easy it is to think of ideal spirituality as something done in isolation between the "I" and God. In as much as the early acetic impulse of Christianity was a withdrawal from community, it represented a tendency to yield to this temptation. This does not mean that spirituality precludes withdrawal, reflection, and personal prayer, but rather that none of these practices can or should ever be divorced from responsibility for creation and reconciled communion with others. God is not to be communed with simply and only in isolation, at least not for the Hebrews who gave shape to these stories. For these Hebrews the call was always back to community even if it involved the pain of vocation. In fact the loss of connection with God is described in Genesis 3 as linked exactly to the loss of communion among humans and creation. The communal task of the pain of childbirth and the sweat of the brow is where God's call of grace sends humankind. Even in the midst of this painful return to community there is hopeful God-redeemed technology–"the Lord God made coats of skin and clothed them." As mentioned above, this act of covering the human predicament is perhaps one of the most profound expressions of grace in the biblical narrative. God covers our shameful self-absorption to make loving community possible.

The implications of the painful call back to community for those called to Christian leadership and the spiritual journey are multi-dimensional. The reality is that in our faith communities we are deeply tainted by the processes of selfish hiding, blaming and fear. In this sense we never escape the curse of Genesis 3. Leaders too, confronted with these realities, will hide, blame and fear. In this context we grasp of easy techniques and technologies (fig leaves) to solve our problem while the real call is one to repentant engagement for community with one another and creation. As we live in a culture dominated by mastery through various techniques we can easily strive to escape the hard work, the sweat-of-our-brow work and the pain-of-birth work of community. Our response to God's individual call can easily end in excuses and blaming. Most of all, we can make call and even spirituality into something in service of the "I".

On Call and Theology

Anselm of Canterbury (1033-1109) taught us that theology is faith seeking understanding. We can also describe it as reading the bible in the present. Whereas both these definition approach theology as rooted in God as subject, Brueggemann points out that there is also another kind of theology encapsulated in the story of Genesis 3, the theology of the snake. There is a subtle shift in this kind of theology in which God becomes in object rather than the subject. Theology is no longer encapsulated in a relationship of trust with God (covenant faithfulness) but rather in analysis and calculation[38]. Mastery and technique, the roots of modern Western culture, are expressed in analysis and calculation. The spirit of such mastery is easily transferred to the community of faith and to the objects of God's call. Later we will see how important it is that God remains the subject and not the object of theology. We are first constituted and addressed by God, not the other way round.

Mastery and technique are also the essential dimensions of contemporary approaches to education. Formation for ministry thus easily degenerates in snake like theology, rather than the hard work of facing the challenge of community. Elsewhere I have argued that the drive to mastery in contemporary western culture and its digital counterpart is reshaping our consciousness[39]. Any approach to forming people for Christian spirituality will have to take great care in attending to the challenge the biblical story of faith poses to the fundamental direction of our culture.

On Call and Freedom

Besides describing humankind as created for community, the Genesis narratives also describe humankind as being free within a covenant of limitation. The kind of freedom described here is not a philosophical freedom to do whatever the autonomous human being fancies. The freedom described here exists within the parameters of God's creative purpose. In Genesis 2 it is usually described in terms of vocation (to serve and to protect the earth), permission/freedom (to eat of all), and prohibition/limit (do not eat of one tree). However, we should hasten to add that Genesis 2 adds another element to this freedom by finishing the story with creation of the woman. It appears that the freedom described here is a freedom in relationship, a freedom to share life, a freedom to be only complete in relation to another. This is both a freedom and a limitation. The human is not whole without the other and we can add the human is not free without the other. True freedom, in this vision, is only possible in dependence on God and one another.

We need not take this relational freedom described in terms of man and woman as a kind of absolute gendered completeness. From a theological perspective we can observe that gender does not extend to God. Even though man and woman by implication form community which is the image of God, the gendered human condition does not define the Divine dimension of community. In fact gender is to a large extent a construction of our cultural worlds rather than a divine given. Yes, there are biological differences, but that is not the point, the point is that people and creation thrive when people and creation no matter their biology live in life giving community of love. There are many levels on which freedom in relationship can make human beings whole. It is not biology that is the issue as much as it is openness to relationship and being in relationship. The good demonstration is the new community of women and men that Jesus formed. These followers defined the call to community in fresh ways and led to the famous Pauline formulation of unity despite difference (Galatians 3:28). These relational dimensions of God and their implications for Christian spirituality will be explored later.

On Call and Suffering

"When Christ calls a man he bids him come and die.[40]"
   (Dietrich Bonhoeffer)

These words penned by Dietrich Bonhoeffer in the shadow of the Nazi regime and in anticipation of his own martyrdom dramatically underline the last aspect of reflection necessary as we consider the character of call to Christian spirituality. The individual call, born out of God's agonising call in the garden, delivers both grace and death. Any call to community in the condition East of Eden challenge us as human beings with death. The image in the Genesis 3 story is dramatic. Cherubim and flaming sword keeps the road to the Tree of Life closed. Yet, at the same time, the narrative unfolds with grace that overwhelms

God-forsaken death. It is not physical dying that is spoken of here. That kind of dying seems to be part of the original order of creation. Life waxes and wanes. Creation itself and its creatures grow old, die and is renewed. The Garden of Eden contains a tree called the Tree of Life for that very reason. Full and meaningful life is still part of the promise; it is unrealised but potentially there in the garden. The tension of call as it unfolds in the stories that are to follow is between the unrealised gracious potential of life, and the desperate God-forsakenness of death.

The New Testament Gospel stories pick up this narrative in the shadow of the cross of Christ. The Gospels paint a Christ on his way to Jerusalem and inexorably on his way to death. This process is dramatically emphasised in the call to death that Jesus extends to his disciples, "Those who love their own life will lose it; those who hate their own life in this world will keep it for life eternal. Whoever wants to serve me must follow me...[41]" It is clear here that this is not first of all a morbid call, rather, it is a call to transform the patterns of God-forsaken death to patterns of grace-filled God-present life. Such transformation and a call to this transformation is painful and contain suffering. There is no individual call, East of Eden that is not a call to some kind of suffering. Yet, the suffering is understood to be in the context of the overwhelming power of God's grace. To reiterate again in Breuggemann's words: "When the facts warrant death, God insists on life for his creatures."

The conditions of "death" are definitively stated in the Genesis 3 narrative. It includes moving away from fidelity to God's creative call to a rhetoric of analysis and calculation. It finds itself acting out of fear with solutions of human mastery, technology and technique based in human autonomy. It hides from community and moves from community to an emphasis on the "I". The Genesis narratives are, "A commentary on human autonomy and how human autonomy without boundaries lead to death[42]." The call to discipleship, which is a kind of call to die, is a call to suffer by denying or turning our back on the autonomy of death while turning towards community and the sharing of life. Later we will see that the early Christians developed the concept of "white martyrdom" or white witness to capture a profound dedication of our lives to God in willing service. This monastic ideal will be instructive as we explore formation for Christian spirituality.

For theological formation for Christian spirituality the call to suffering confronts those called with the power of death. In addition it implies preparation for suffering and the formation of a community of support for those called.

Conclusion

We have established here that the Call of God is fundamental to all creation and to our condition as human beings. As the world is called into being so we are called ones. For us to grasp our call we are required to listen. Christian spirituality requires us to listen. Listening in anticipation for action and listening on the way of actions is the fundamental disposition of Christian spirituality. It is therefore to listening that we now turn.

Notes

1. Placher, W.C. *Callings: Twenty Centuries of Christian Vocation* Grand Rapids: William B. Eerdmans Publishing Company, 2005, 210.

2. There is a large literature on this, see for example, a particularly fine argument by Judith Butler, in *Bodies That Matter: On the Discursive Limits of Sex.* New York: Routledge, 1993.

3. Purves, A. *Pastoral Theology in the Classical Tradition.* Knoxville: Westminster/John Knox Press, 2001), 12.

4. Ibid.. 13.

5. Ibid., 34.

6. Brown, P. *Augustine of Hippo: A Biography* Berkley: University of California Press, 1969, 139.

7. Ibid., 138.

8. Placher, Ibid., 39.

9. Ibid., 68.

10. Ibid., 10.

11. I use Breuggemann's commentary on Genesis in the Interpretation series liberally but advisedly. Breuggemann is a provocative author that stimulates creative thought and expanding exegesis. He is therefore a wonderful muse for a theologian, although Biblical scholars do not always appreciate this creativity! My approach here is to use his provocative arguments, but also to balance them with the perspectives of other Biblical scholars.

12. Breuggemann, W. *Genesis: Interpretation - A Bible Commentary for Teaching and Preaching* Atlanta: John Knox Press, 1982, 1. In addition, it must be noted that Gordon J. Wenham argues that the primeval history of Genesis 1-11 "serves to enhance the appreciation of the patriarchs and their calling" Wenham, G.J. *Word Biblical Commentary. Genesis 1-15.* Nashville: Thomas Nelson, 1987, lii.

13. Ibid.

14. Elsewhere I have argued that a biblical hermeneutic for the 21st century church should be rooted in the mission of God, in solidarity with the poor, in a life-giving and liberating Christ-focused praxis, in a community of the Spirit, in discernment of the spirits, in missional repentance, and in a doxology and *poiesis* for wholeness. Fensham, C.J. *Emerging from the Dark Age Ahead: The Future of the North American Church.* Toronto: Clements Academic, 2011, 42-52.

15. Ibid., 10.

16. Some scholars trace large parts of the origin of the book of Genesis to the time of exile in Babylon. See Breuggemann, Ibid., 25. Others argue for the substance of the text coming together much earlier. See Wenham, Ibid., xliii-xlv. In both cases the polemic against Sumerian and Babylonian myths is important to notice. As Wenham puts it, "It is affirming the unity of God in the face of polytheism, his justice, rather than caprice, his power as opposed to his impotence,

his concern for mankind rather than his exploitation. And, whereas Mesopotamia clung to the wisdom of primeval man, Genesis records his sinful disobedience." Ibid., l.

17. Ibid., 13.

18. Ibid., 18.

19. Breuggemann, Ibid., 34 & Sailhamer, J.H. *The Pentateuch as Narrative: A Biblical-Theological Commentary.* Grand Rapids: Zondervan, 1992, 97-98.

20. Barth, K. *Church Dogmatics III., I.* T & T Clark, 1977, 183-187.

21. Kearney, Richard *On Stories.* New York: Routgledge, 2002, 3.

22. See Fensham, C.J. *Towards Narrative Pastoral Grief Counselling: Reflections on a Case Study of the Grief Journey of a father and His Family.* Waterloo: Wilfrid Laurier University. 1994. Unpublished Th.M.Thesis.

23. Quoted in Placher, Ibid., 1.

24. Kearney, Ibid., 4.

25. Kearny refers to Dilthey's concept of Zusammenhang des Lebens literally, "the hanging together of our lives", Ibid.

26. See a detailed discussion of the issues in translation and interpretation around the first three verses of Genesis 1 in Wenham, Ibid., 5-18.

27. Ibid., 12.

28. The need to form stories to make sense of human actions and life (*praxis*) is described by modern phenomenological philosophers such as Heidegger as "retrieval" and "the project of being towards an end."   Ibid., 129.

29. It is very important to recognise that there is an essential difference between this understanding of Christian spirituality and story, and the existential philosophies that developed in the 19th and 20th century. In fact much of popular individualist Christian spirituality bears more resemblance to the structure of individualism developed in these philosophies than to the biblical narratives and their meaning.

30. Form the Hymn: "You are Called to Tell the Story" by Ruth Duck in, *The Book of Praise. Hymn 583.* Montreal: The Presbyterian Church in Canada, 1997, 756.

31. John Calvin put it this way, "First, we must attend to what a sacrament is. It seems to me, then, a simple and appropriate definition to say, that it is an external sign, by which the Lord seals on our consciences his promises of good-will toward us, in order to sustain the weakness of our faith, and we in our turn testify our piety towards him, both before himself, and before angels as well as men. We may also define more briefly by calling it a testimony of the divine favour toward us, confirmed by an external sign, with a corresponding attestation of our faith towards Him. You may make your choice of these definitions, which in meaning differ not from that of Augustine, which defines a sacrament to be a visible sign of a sacred thing, or a visible form of an invisible grace, but does not contain a better or surer explanation." Calvin, J. *The Institutes of the Christian Religion. Book IV* translated by H. Beverage (Grand Rapids: Eerdmans, 1957) 2492. From a Roman Catholic perspective Avery Dulles offers this definition of the sacrament: "A sacrament is a socially constituted or communal symbol of the presence of grace coming to fulfillment." Dulles, A.R. *Models of the Church* New York: Doubleday, 1991, 59.

32. Van Selms, A. *De Prediking van het Oude Testament: Genesis deel I.* Nijkerk: Uitgeverij G.F. Callenbach. 1967, 36. See also Wenham's extensive discussion of the concept "image of God" in which he also notes the possible reading of this term as "shadow", Ibid., 29-32.

33. Breuggemann, Ibid., 2

34. Ibid., 50.

35. Ibid., 37 The text here also carries the sense of creation working the way it should - being right.

36. Ibid.

37. Ibid., 49

38. Ibid., 48

39. Fensham, 2008, Ibid.

40. Bonhoeffer, D. *The Cost of Discipleship.* London: SCM/Canterbury Press, 2001, 44.
41. John 12:25-26 *Good News Bible*
42. Breuggemann, Ibid., 52.

2

Listen

"But the word is very near you, in your mouth and in your heart, so that you may do it."

–(THE TORAH – DOCUMENT OF THE COVENANT – DEUTERONOMY, 30:14 NASB)

Batter my heart, three person'd God; for, you
As yet but knocke, breathe, shine, and seeke to mend;

–(JOHN DONNE 1572-1631)

It is all about God. God comes first and then we can consider ourselves as creatures of God. This means that God is the subject and we are the work of God's creative word. We are God's audience and our primary posture is to listen. The great unfolding story of call and vocation that we explored in the previous chapter unfolds through this dramatic theme of both Hebrew and Christian Scriptures. It proclaims the story of God's faithfulness to God's covenant for the blessing of all nations and for the whole of creation. In his exploration of the theme of justification in Pauline writing N.T. Wright describes theme as, "God's-single-plan-through-Israel-for-the-world"[1] John Donne, in his poem above, expressed the true posture of listening and being acted upon by the faithful "three person'd God[2]." Freedom is to be found when we stand, listen and respond within this story. It is in the listening disposition when addressed by God and when we grasp the freedom of God's limitation that we can be truly free. In the unfolding story of Christian spirituality, we are called first, and we are then to listen attentively as we join the journey on which the calling Creator God invites us.

Listening for God's Call to Mission

The Mission

I will never forget the first course I attended on the historical background to the Hebrew Scriptures. A few weeks into the course the professor reached the story of Abraham. He was unusually animated that day, he spoke of the absolute wonder of this seminal story in the unfolding narrative of the Hebrew Scriptures. This man from Ur in Balylonia, at advanced age, heard God's call, and wonder of wonders he responded! The professor's enthusiasm was infectious. Here is a story that captured God's gracious plan for creation in a nutshell. The professor, who was a person of deep faith as well as a world recognised researcher, peaked my interest in the uniqueness of faith displayed in this story even though the story never explicitly mentions faith. He also made me realise that there is a challenging and sacrificial dimension to call.

In chapter 1 we reflected on vocation in terms of God's call. In this chapter, as we develop the idea of vocation as listening, we will focus on God's purpose – what we will call *The Mission of God*. What is the meaning of creation? If call and promise play such critical roles in the founding stories of creation, where is it all leading? What is the call for? What are we called to be and do? At the heart of the life of faith is the belief that creation is meaningful. This means that the reality in which we exist is unfolding towards a purpose. In chapter 1 the idea of purpose and direction was already signalled with the concept eschatology. We also discussed the way the creation story in Genesis 2 reflects the meaning of the purpose of humankind in creation as being those who are meant to serve and protect the garden and thus protect serve and protect creation. In fact the same words used in Genesis 2 to describe how humans are to serve and protect the garden and the earth are the words used for worship and faithfulness to God. Serving and protecting creation is inseparable from devotion to God.

The dimensions of meaning and purpose take on a new role with the story of human rebellion in Genesis 3. In this narrative, God's call is a call to return to the original intention of human care for creation. The humans in the story, and by extension all humankind including you and I, are called to turn and return. Turning and returning to God and God's task for us is traditionally called repentance in Christian language. The act of listening begins by hearing the call to repentance. For most of Christian history public worship included listening to a call to repentance and responding in penance and praise. We dispense with this tradition at our peril. However, for a very long time Christians only heard the call to repentance in terms of a return to God through Jesus Christ without understanding that this movement and turn of reconciliation puts us on a path that is to tend and care for creation and one another. In short our repentance was often isolated and individualised to the point of losing the larger task set before us. We can demonstrate the pattern of turning and acting on the call of God for the good of all creation by referring to the story of Noah.   In the call of Noah there is a focus on a salvific and healing task for Noah and humankind. But, this task includes not just humankind, but also other creatures. Thus God's purpose continues to be the thriving of all creation and Noah has a key role to re-establish this thriving community of creatures.

Noah's task as the one to take care of God's creatures and to re-establish their place demonstrates the content of biblical stewardship. In contrast, "stewardship", in our enlightenment and industrial culture has become associated with exploitation and use of resources and a drive to machine-like efficiency. Stewardship, in this warped sense, means getting the most out of earth's resources for our own benefit. To walk the way of Christian spirituality is to understand that stewardship in the sense of the book of Genesis is a caring for creation, a fostering of health and wholeness, on behalf of God the creator. To be spiritual is to act in such sustaining and caring ways towards God's creation. The matter and stuff of creation – the animals, plants and ecological systems – are all part of a vibrant living reality wherein we stand with the awesome power to destroy or to protect. God's mission for us is inextricably linked to creation and the care for it. This means that Christian spirituality is by definition an eco-spirituality of responsibility for healing and care. With all the complexities and unanswered questions that came with our understanding of the evolutionary process of the universe and the earth we do know that we have emerged as humans with a fearsome ability to destroy creation as well as with a considerable ability, if we wish, to protect it.

As we keep listening to the stories of the Book of Genesis we discover that after the story of the Tower of Babel, there is the dramatic break between Genesis 11:32 and 12:1.   Here there is a shift from the history of humankind as a whole to the particular history of Israel.[3] By Genesis 12, with the story of Abraham, the story unfolds in more detail and with a distinctiveness of call focused on Abraham and his descendants. In Genesis 12:1-3 this call and its blessing are made very clear. The rich formative and metaphorical power of this key biblical narrative and its many dimensions keep echoing through the whole of the Bible and through history and its importance cannot be overstated. If we wish to listen for God's call and listen for an explanation of God's mission this is where we have to be particularly attentive. The Christian spiritual journey is always in some way contained within the journey from Abram to Abraham. Abram becomes Abraham, in his response to God's call. In listening and turning to God's journey he gains identity and meaning as a person. Likewise, Christian spirituality rests on the key discovery of hearing God call us into being and granting us a special place and special meaning in creation.

In his commentary on Genesis 12, Walter Breuggemann refers to the first mission of God in "calling the worlds into being".[4] If we want to listen for the *Mission of God*, we want to do so by first recognising that God moves beyond Godself in a loving mission of creation. In this act of creation God gives of Godself and also in some way limits Godself. Perhaps this is a very difficult thought to ponder? We need to imagine what things might have been like before creation when God simply was and is. In our imagination we could capture a sense of God being all in all and everywhere in everywhere. For God to make something that is different from God implies that God in some way limits this unlimited and perhaps infinite being of Godself. This act of making and limiting Godself is an act of sacrificial love. In as much as we can grasp this at all, it is love that overflows out of the joyous loving union of the inner life of God! For creation to come into being God has to give up something and somewhere. This does not necessarily mean that God needs creation to love, for God's love given from Father to Son to Spirit and vice versa is sufficient. Yet this love is so abundant that it moves God to create. God's mission begins with this act of overflowing love that creates something that can stand beside God and stand in relationship with God. God can treasure, cherish, and admire creation. Creation comes from God, bears God's mark, but is not the same as God. The word mission is from the Latin *mittere* which means to send. This move of God in creation can be described as a kind of Divine act of overflowing sending forth – mission. The Creative Word speaks forth creation and this is the heart of mission. Traditionally theologians have spoken of these acts of God beyond God's inner life as the economy of God. Everything we say about spirituality after this basic insight has to be said against the backdrop of the economy of God's original mission of creation.

In the act of creation God is clearly the subject. By that we mean that God is the one who acts and who is the most important part of the story. Yet even as it is God acting and creating, God's relationship with creation is not described as a withdrawn Subject but as God intimately involved in and with creation. The wind of God that moves over the deep waters or the dark void in Genesis 1 comes from God and becomes involved with creation. With the creation of the human being God's breath (wind – *Ruah*) is what gives life. God thus does not stand simply over and away from creation but as subject that is also in an intimate way connected with creation – the object. It is neither possible to confuse God with creation, nor is it possible to remove God from it. Creation lives and moves and has its being in God. God is not simply the Subject, God is also "walking a way" with creation – to speak metaphorically[5]. This is already evident in the pleasure God takes in creation ("and God saw that it was good[6]"), and the care with which God engages creation and humankind in particular. God is not dispassionate, but moved by the actions of the creatures. Why else do we find God cherishing and blessing creation on the Sabbath and God's haunting call to the humans in the garden – "Where?" As Christians on our journey with God we are always God's objects, God is not our object to be studied and pronounced upon. Doing that would be doing the theology of the snake in the garden. Christian spirituality means that we are objects of a God who is deeply engaged with our lives and our plight, a God who calls us back to our original intent as carers of the Garden, a God that seeks to stand in relationship with us as we stand in relationship with one another and creation.

The idea that God is somehow so beyond creation that God is essentially untouched by the plight of creation is described in traditional theological language as the *impassability* of God. The Hebrew conception of God that we encounter in Genesis does not know such an "impassable" God. There is only one God here, but this God is not a distant monotheistic God, but rather a God-in-community – a God of relationship. In Genesis this relational dimension of God is expressed by the concept covenant – a concept well known and fundamental to the legal systems of the ancient Near East. The solemn agreement between God the Creator and the called one, combined with God's unfailing faithfulness to God's covenant, becomes the theme that plays behind all other themes in both the Hebrew and Christian Scriptures. Through covenant God binds Godself to creation and, in the Christian understanding of the covenant, in Jesus the Messiah God enters creation for its redemption. In this act – the *Mission of God* in the Messiah – God demonstrates even more clearly that God is the loving missioning God *for* creation[7]. We can say that John 3:16 is thus one of the most concise and profound summaries of the whole story of the Hebrew and Christian Scriptures – "God so loved *the world* (cosmos) that God gave God's only begotten Son…" (my emphasis) This act demonstrates the depth of the love and faithfulness of the Creator towards creation. In contrast, the human side of this covenant, the side in which humans and Israel fail continually, demonstrates the human propensity to respond inadequately in contrast to God's willingness to join humankind in this plight by responding properly in Jesus the Messiah – the God-man.

Are these ways of understanding too complex and mind boggling to be of practical use in the Christian life? No! It is extremely important that we listen and know who we are before God if we want to walk the way of God and join the mission of God to which we are called. Letting the stories of Genesis enrich our imagination is no idle ivory tower exercise. It is the very intent of these stories to let us know our destiny in creation. The call that we have explored in the first chapter is a call to mission. It is this mission of the covenant now led by the Messiah that is the content of the mission to which we are called. It is this same mission of the covenant for which we are to be shaped as people of God. This brings us back to that all-important, but by no means the only covenant in the Bible – the covenant of God with Abraham.

What does God promise and what does God require? What are the terms of the covenant? To what is Abraham invited to agree and what does this mean for us? The first hints are already to be found in Genesis 12. As Breuggemann reflects theologically on the unfolding of this narrative he points to the problem of barrenness in Abram and Sarah and God's speech to this barren family. They are called out of their native land to abandonment, renunciation and relinquishment. Barrenness becomes a metaphor for the consequence of human rebellion and hubris. The word, Breuggemann observes, falls hard on the ears of our contemporary culture. Renunciation is the very opposite of our self-indulgent consumer culture. Yet, the command is not a law or discipline, but rather rooted in promise for freedom and fulfillment. To find the way out of barrenness, the command to relinquishment, is the only way out. This invitation to forsake all for the covenant mission is reflected in Jesus' own covenantal command "…whoever loses his life for my sake and the gospel's will save it."[8] From this reflection on the original Abrahamic call to covenant we can argue that our call to the mission of the covenant is indeed also a deeply counter cultural call. The call of formation for Christian spirituality is one that calls us *away from* our own barrenness, our own meaninglessness, and our own pursuit of self-satisfaction. However, with joy we discover that this call is also a promise. The call away from barrenness brings us to freedom.

Behind the command that leads to promise, plays the theme of a call from barrenness – a metaphor for the consequence of sin. Grace in this covenant call is expressed as God cancels the consequences of human autonomy with promised gifts. God asserts five promises in God's call to covenant, God will *make* Abram, God will *bless* Abram, God will *magnify* Abram's name, God will *bless those who bless* Abram, and God will *curse those who disdain* Abram.[9] Here God's self-assertion contrasts and cancels the human self-assertion in the garden and anticipates the human failure to respond adequately to the covenant. God's promise to Abram emphasises that we are not the absolute and autonomous people that we imagined we are, we are not what the theologian Karl Barth called "absolute man", we will not make ourselves, we will not bring blessing to ourselves, we will not magnify our own names, we will not be able to convey blessing ourselves, and we will not be able to curse those who disdain us. These promises from God also neatly and graciously contrast and *return* the things that Adam and Eve lose in the garden. To use Gospel language, the losing of life is the gaining of that life. The losing of our security in place and family is gaining land and family. The losing of honour and name is the gaining of those things as God's gift. The losing of protection and security is gaining those things in God's protection. We can say that the long-standing tradition of Christian spirituality expressed in the two movement of relinquishing one's life (mortification) and gaining one life (vivification) is already present right here in Genesis 12:1-3. The call to the mission of vocation is a call to relinquishment that ultimately receives all that we crave from God. However, the gift of the promise of the covenant is not a self-indulgent gift. Walter Breuggemann puts it this way,

> The well-being of Israel carried potential for the well-being of other nations. Israel is never permitted to live in a vacuum. It must always live with, for, and among the others. The barren ones are now mandated for the needs of the others.[10]

In Genesis 12:3 the well-being of Abraham and his family – Israel – thus becomes linked to the well-being of all peoples of the earth. Scholars debate among themselves just how passively to translate verse 3. It is therefore interesting to find that Gordon Wenham makes a strong argument that the text should be read as a culmination of the argument about Abraham that leads to a translation that reads, "all families of the earth will find blessing in you."[11]
The promise of Abram's prolific offspring in whom all families will be blessed is a reiteration of the original creation blessing and imperative found in Genesis 1:28.[12] The call is to this blessing of "all families" which, in the Christian Gospel becomes "all nations" (*panta ta ethne* in the Greek language of the New Testament). Of course what all this means for our understanding of Christian spirituality is that there is not spirituality simply for the edification of the "I" as an individual. Even though I am blessed as a person and loved and embraced by God, my blessing is meant to be conveyed to the nations and to the world. This is a sobering thought in the light of so much contemporary Christian spirituality focused on individualistic benefits rather than the task of blessing others.

God's covenant with Abraham and his family is more fully set out in Genesis 15. This chapter in the Torah is pivotal both for the tradition of Judaism and for Christianity. It has been described as the oldest statement of Abrahamic faith, and as we will see a little later, it is also the seminal text for the theology of Paul.[13] I site the full text here because it is so important:

> After this, Abram had a vision and heard the LORD say to him, "Do not be afraid, Abram. I will shield you from danger and give you a great reward." But Abram answered, "Sovereign LORD, what good will your reward do me, since I have no children .... The LORD took him outside and said, "Look at the sky and try to count the stars; you will have as many descendants as that." Abram put his trust in the LORD, and because of this the LORD was pleased with him and accepted him. (*From Genesis 15, GNB*)

There is of course much that can be discussed around the origin and meaning of different elements of this chapter. For the sake of our exploration here one matter stands out in importance. This is the matter of the contrast between this covenant made by God with Abraham and the later covenants of Sinai and Deuteronomy. Wenham describes this contrast thus,

> The Sinaitic and Deuteronomic covenants were agreements imposing obligations on both God and Israel: their closest extra-biblical analogy is found in the ancient international treaties made by great powers with their vassals. This covenant with Abraham is different: it is a promissory oath made by God alone.[14]

This difference in the core covenant and core promise behind the unfolding Biblical narrative is not without theological significance. In this narrative the initiative of God carries all the force. We can echo again Breuggemann's assertion about the Genesis narrative in general, "When the facts warrant death, God insists on life for his creatures."[15] That God is the primary subject of the covenant is clear. There is a response from Abraham, but this response fits clearly in the text as secondary to God's promissory oath that drives the story. Abraham's faith is also noted and emphasised in the narrative. We encounter this emphasis in Abraham's silence in the face of God's promise in verses 5-6. The silence warrants an editorial explanation in verse 6, "And he believed in the Lord and it was counted to him as righteousness."[16] This editorial comment clarifies the question that Abraham poses in verse 8, "...how am I to know...?", and emphasises that Abraham's questions and doubtful objections are outweighed by his trust in God's promise despite all appearances. This word "believe" that we find in Genesis 15:6, which later becomes a key concept in the theology of Paul, can mean: relying on someone, to give credence to a message or to trust someone.[17] In fact Paul quotes this verse in Romans (Rom 4:3) and it becomes the backbone of his theology of justification.

Breuggemann notes that the gift of faith in Abraham's life is in response to the "sign" of the many stars in the sky to which God points (verse 5).[18] This, Breuggemann argues, is not proof or demonstration, but rather, sacrament – a visible sign of invisible grace. The word sacrament is derived from the Latin rendering of the Greek word for mystery. The gift of faith unveils the full hope of the mystery of the sign. The sacramentality of the covenant is further enforced by the covenant ritual that follows later in the chapter. This ritual includes body, blood, awe and fire. The call to covenant mission unfolds through promise, objection that the promise is not realised, sacrament, faith and then awe. In this sense we can say the call to vocation is always fundamentally sacramental. We do not hear and respond to God's call out of a proven promise, but out of a promise accompanied by a sign of God's grace (sacrament) that often does not appear self-evident in our experience. There is something in call that requires risk, courage, and trust in the face of all evidence to the contrary. This sense of risk, courage and trust against all evidence makes the marks of a Christian journey of spirituality.

It is critical for our understanding of Christian spirituality to discern what is meant by the concept *righteousness* in Genesis 15:6 (the Hebrew word is *tsedawkaw*). Abraham's righteousness is a pivotal part of the story of his call. What is meant by this term and what could it mean for us who are called? The Old Testament scholar Gordon Wenham, after discussing different theories and noting the "righteousness" in the Pentateuch usually means God-pleasing action, argues that in Gen 15:6 righteousness has the particular meaning that God *judges* that Abraham's response is the right one in relation to God's revelation.[19] This does not negate in any way the message clearly expounded throughout the Old Testament that faith leads to righteous action, but it does place the emphasis on God's judgement as a key element of the declaration of righteousness. We shall see that this particular emphasis in Genesis 15 has important implications for our reading of Paul in the New Testament and for our understanding of the meaning of call, faith and righteousness. As these three themes are woven together in the story of the call of Abraham, so they are important for our own stories of call and vocation.

At the beginning of this chapter I referred to N.T. Wright's work on the place of this covenant as central in the theology of Paul.[20] Wright argues convincingly that behind the word *righteousness* (*dikaiosyne* and its different forms in the Greek), in Paul's letters lies the central concept of God's covenant faithfulness. In addition, Wright argues that the concept of justification by faith in

Paul's theology is impacted by the idea that righteousness is in the first place a judgement about human beings made by God. The argument of Old Testament scholars examined above supports this claim. Among other things Wright shows how the key covenant chapters in the Torah, Genesis 15 and Deuteronomy 30, inform all Paul's thinking with great consistency. When this insight is combined with what has now been discovered about the world-view, debates, and cultural context wherein Paul operated (often referred to as first century Judaism), it is clear that Paul thought of Jesus as the Messiah, the one true Israelite that finally fulfills the covenant of God with Abraham. This, Wright argues, becomes for Paul the *righteousness* of Jesus the Messiah. True to the prophetic tradition that described the covenant failure of Israel in dramatic Hebrew court style, Paul too imagines the great court case of God against the failure of Israel to fulfil the covenant. God's judgement on Jesus the Messiah, as in the case with God's judgement on the response of Abraham, is that the covenant is righteously fulfilled. Now in Jesus the Messiah, the covenant is finally fulfilled, the day of the Lord has begun, the resurrection has proven Jesus truly faithful, and in him and through him the covenant promise is now being realised. The divine judgement on Jesus the Messiah is yet again: "He is righteous" despite all the dark events of the passion to the contrary. The resurrection is proof of this divine declaration of righteousness. Yet again, as in the book of Genesis, when the facts seemed to demand death, God chose life for God's creatures...

What are the implications for Christian spirituality of such a Divine judgement on Jesus the Messiah? We need to note that Jesus the Messiah, is of Abraham's family and is described as the Son of God, and perfectly fulfils the covenant on our behalf. The parallels with the five reversals of the Abrahamic blessing explored above are striking. He relinquishes all in trust of the Father. He gives up security and honour for complete dishonour on a Roman cross. He seeks not for himself but for the well-being of all. He enters the captivity of the final enemy – death. In all these ways his actions are the opposite of "absolute humankind" or Adam. And here is the kicker; by blessing him we are blessed with the verdict of righteousness. By entering his new community that includes all nations, all genders, all stations in life without discrimination we become the "all families" blessed through him. The resurrected Jesus the Messiah becomes the sacrament of God for us.[21] Like Abraham in the original covenant described in Genesis 15, in awe we behold the vastness of God's blessing in the body and the blood. Despite all experience to the contrary we trust the promise of God and we do so not just for ourselves but for the benefit of all creation. The call to a Christian spiritual journey and formation for ministry proceeds from these insights. In the words of Bonhoeffer, "the call to discipleship is a call to die."[22] We should add to that the Genesis account tells us that a call to die is a call to full and meaningful life that becomes life giving to others and creation.

This train of thought brings us at last to the tension between the promise of God and the already and the not-yet of its fulfilment in history and in our experience. Any person walking in the way of Christ will find a certain experience of barrenness, hopes unrealised and ideals disappointed. Abraham, no stranger to such disappointments, had some valid questions in the face of God's call and promise. Abraham's question, "Sovereign Lord, how am I to know…?" reflects our own overwhelming experience in the face of a world that is warped, hurting, and being destroyed. We ask how am I to know when we face the great questions of theodicy (how could a good God permit evil?) or the senseless suffering of the hungry and the destitute. We face the same question when cancer strikes down a person. We face it when we see the tempting power of human mastery through technology. We pose Abraham's question when it seems that there is too little evidence of God's coming kingdom in our world. Abraham's question is essentially the question, "why must it be so?" Why are all the promises not fully realised? Why the waiting and the suffering? Why, to put it in Paul's words, do "we know that up to the present time all of creation groans with pain, like the pain of childbirth."?[23] Christian spirituality will lead to such questions and the constant challenge they pose at every turn. As with Abraham our experience may yet offer but a dim shimmer of the fullness of God's promise to come. Walking the way that God calls is what is called "walking by faith" in the great biblical chapter on faith – Hebrews 11.

The questions raised by what is promised and expected yet not yet experienced are discussed in Christian theology under the name eschatology. Eschatology is a word that speaks of the last things or the things of the end. N.T. Wright's work on the place of eschatology and the work of the Holy Spirit in Paul's argument for the fulfilment of the covenant in Jesus the Messiah is most helpful in helping us understand eschatology and Christian spirituality. Wright's argument shows how Paul deals with the difficult questions raised above. How did Paul understand the discrepancy between the arrival of Jesus the Messiah, and the not-yet experience of the fulfilment of the promises of the covenant? How do those with faith function in the midst of the experience of evil, suffering and struggle while maintaining trust in God who has brought reconciliation in the Messiah? This question is echoed today by the more modern struggle with theodicy and protest atheism[24]. Paul did not frame the question in the same way as we might today, yet he writes to the early Christian communities to address their experience of the incongruity between experience and expectation. For Paul this is consistently expressed in terms of raising theological questions in a pastoral way focused on the context of the local community. Paul's response deals with these thorny questions by pointing to the nature of the Christian community – the church. By going in this direction Paul affirms the goal of the covenant that moves towards the blessing of all nations and the reconciliation of all things in creation which is achieved partly through and in the Christian community. He responds to the persistence of evil and suffering by pointing towards God's final judgement that is still to come. God is a relational covenant God. Without a community in relationship and covenant, redemption cannot fully unfold. This move by Paul deftly refocuses local Christian communities in his time to attend to the struggle to integrate Jew and Gentile, male and female, and rich and poor. Diversity in relationship, rather than a problem, becomes for Paul the mission and badge of the covenant fulfilled in Christian community. Even the great theological arguments made through Paul's letters (and other letters in sympathy with his writing), serve to reinforce this fundamental theology of God's covenant with the particular (Abraham and his family) for the universal blessing of all peoples and all things. Wright gently points out that it does not serve us well to separate this larger agenda of Paul from the other great doctrinal statements contained in his work, he writes,

> Any attempt to give an account of a doctrine which screens out the call of Israel, the gift of the Spirit and/or the redemption of all creation is doomed to be less than fully biblical.[25]

It is thus critical to understand how Paul describes the tension between the already of the Messiah and the not yet of God's covenant fulfilment. Wright argues that at the heart of Paul's response to this tension lies Paul's understanding of the work of the Holy Spirit in the community of faith and in the believer. This understanding of the Spirit is Trinitarian in nature in the sense of an implicit Trinitarian understanding, particularly because Paul understood the work of the Father, the Messiah and the Spirit of the Messiah as inseparable. Wright concludes,

> Paul invites his hearers to trust *both* in Jesus Christ *and* in the Father whose love triumphed in the death of his Son-*and in the Holy Spirit who makes that victory operative in our moral lives and who enables us to love God in return.*[26]

For Wright it is clear that Paul, when it comes to this eschatological function of the Holy Spirit, understood the Spirit as the Spirit of the Son.[27] If the community of faith believes in the fulfillment of the covenant in the Messiah, and if it now lives in the "already" of the verdict of justification before God in the Messiah, while also living in the face of sin, suffering, and failure that still persists, it does so eschatologically as it lives in the Holy Spirit that makes transformation possible while the community awaits the final day of the Lord. The life of the Messiah becomes possible in the Christian community by being in the Spirit of the Son. In this community we live in the Spirit so that we are truly free.

In response to listening to the argument above, our mission, and our formation for Christian spirituality can now be located in this theological place-the place of the work of the Spirit of the Son. As we listen to these ancient letters written to communities very different from our own, living in a world strange and different from ours, we can listen also for the echoes of the work of the Spirit that works still in the same way yet in our own unique situation. Even though the challenge of diversity in our situations may be different from first century Palestine, the thrust of the argument remains that our communities and our leadership in them are called to bring together all peoples and all things in the redemption of Jesus the Messiah.

Of particular importance to our "listening" at this point is to re-consider that very challenging and deeply human question outlined earlier, "Why must it be so?" Why has an anticipated and hoped for redemption not fully come? Why suffering? Why a sighing and hurting ecology? Why cancer, disease, war and evil? Why do we need to make this journey? Why do we still need promise and hope? Why is there still a "not yet" to the journey of faith? These are of course questions that touch on unanswerable mystery. Yet, can we see perhaps a glimmer of understanding as we consider the role and place of freedom and process in what we know of the reality of creation? Does a relational creation existing in a relational God require a relational journey open to suffering? Can love only be realised in the midst of the possibility of openness to the limitation that any "other" and "Other" places on us? That is, is love only possible in the face of the real possibility of rejection hate and suffering? Does the scientific story of the earth with all its evolutionary violence and beautiful diverse co-operative thriving fecundity relay a necessity of suffering on the way to love? In some ways these thoughts simply reflect a very old Greek philosophical and later Christian response to the problem of evil. Such glimmerings of understanding do not address all the complexities of suffering, natural and ecological disasters and some of the inherent violence in the evolutionary process. However, they do represent a real dimension that helps us understand why life is a journey towards God and in God that is yet unfinished and challenged by suffering. We will attend more to this as we consider later the issue of the habits of Christian spirituality.

One of the great challenges that Reformation thought left us is the tension between what is considered the gift of God's grace and human action or "good works." This duality has often led Reformed Christians in particular to frown on passages in Paul's letters that seemed to emphasise human effort for good or human effort towards the fruit of the Holy Spirit. One of the findings of the new school of Pauline scholarship, that uncovers the Judaistic dimensions of Paul, is a renewed interest in the seeming lack of tension between Paul's assertions about the gift of redemption as an act of God's grace, and Paul's equal emphasis on concerted human action for a moral life in community. For Paul, or the Pauline author, there does not seem to be a tension between justification as a gift from God in Jesus Christ, and, for example, the strong imperative to "work out your salvation in fear and trembling"(Phil 2:12). In fact, the very next verse in Philippians matches the human effort with God's will at work within the lives and wills of the community of faith. Wright points out that this means that there should not be any lack of effort towards the life that reflects God's covenant and reign. Yet, when that effort is made, its source is ascribed to God, and particularly in Paul's thought, God's work through the Spirit who is the Spirit of the Son.

When the Christian community exerts itself in right living, it is the Spirit and character of Jesus the Messiah that is being expressed and that inspires the effort. As with the findings of research on first century Judaism, God's covenant of grace was understood to precede the law and effort to fulfil the law, so it is to be in the Christian community.[28] God's grace comes in the Messiah Jesus who fulfils the covenant and God judges and declares the community justified through him. Now, the effort of the community to live true to the covenant that brings God's blessings to all peoples and things proceeds from that grace. There is clearly in Paul's thought in continuity with the Judaistic expectation of the judgement of works.[29] In his detailed analysis of Romans 9:30-31 Wright shows that the problem that Paul presents in relation with the law was not Israel's effort towards fulfilling God's law, but rather Israel's attempt to keep the law for self-righteousness.[30] It is rather like the T-shirt I recently saw that claimed, "Jesus died to reserve 'myspace' in heaven". Besides the pun on the social network site, it also betrays the idea of self-interest in following Christ. Rather, Wright convincingly points out, Paul is concerned to show that the intention of the law, and the intention of the Spirit and character of the Messiah is bringing God's blessing to all people and all things. This universal and selfless focus is at the heart of the covenant and its fulfilment. In the early first century Christian communities to whom Paul writes, this is his concern—there can be no division between Jew and Greek, male or female, rich or poor, all are brought into God's covenant community-the church. In addition, Paul holds before them the vision of the ultimate redemption of all things when God will become all in all. In this way the community of faith is different from the world around it. This community begins to embody the fulfilment of the covenant and the signs of the coming reign of God. The unusual life of community in diversity and its witness for the redemption of all things is Paul's concern.

As we listen to this message in the earliest documents of the Christian faith, what does it mean for formation for Christian spirituality? For one thing I would suggest that it means encouraging habits of life and moral behaviour that express our best knowledge of the personality and character of Jesus the Messiah. In particular, it means that our leaders must be formed in ways that encourage the widest inclusion of diversity of peoples and cultures as well as care for the creation in which we live. The spirit in which this is to be done is to be what Paul calls the "fruit of the Spirit." This conclusion means that there is a focus on theological practice in formation that makes up a core and inalienable element of theological formation for ministry. Such practice occurs in community.

The focus on diversity, and the focus on practice plus the focus on community, support the centrality of the quest for righteousness that includes justice in Christian spirituality. In a very basic way the path of Christian spirituality requires formation for justice by joining diverse conversations with others towards justice in our world. This is not some new invention; this journey towards justice in community, as we saw in our discussion of Paul's theology above reflects the very core of his understanding of the Good News of Jesus Christ. The way N.T. Wright unpacks "righteousness" in the New Testament suggests that justice is at its core. We can say that Christian spirituality is only authentic where people quest for righteousness by engaging others for justice. That means that there is something essentially communal and something essentially ethical and something essentially moral about following the way of Jesus Christ in the world. This ethic and moral is about justice and it challenges us to work with others, including those who are fundamentally different than ourselves.

When we live in the world we discover that one of the most basic challenges is to bring together difference. Such difference could include the more mundane experiences such as taste and different perspectives on the same event. It may also include the differences created by gender or sexual orientation, experience and perspective and cultural differences. The challenge of diversity is always captured in the tension between affirming difference and bringing unity and harmony. "Inclusion" can become coercive in its drive towards harmony.

For example we can mean well by saying to someone else "you are just like me". However, that person may really not be "just like me"! "Difference" can become a force for division and conflict. All Christian communities struggle with how to deal with this well. For example, the early community that the Gospel of Matthew was written for struggled with the difference between Jews who became Christians and Gentiles who became Christians. How then can we find a way to practice Christian spirituality that will affirm difference and also bring justice in community and in creation? I suggest that the response to this dilemma should grow out of the normativity of Jesus the Messiah.

Perhaps this sounds too simplistic? Are we not returning to a kind of mindless "what would Jesus do?" mentality that could end up in the absurdities of the "what would Jesus drive?" silliness? We could entertain the objections of Albert Schweitzer and many others that we all tend to find our own comfortable "Jesus" in our reading of the New Testament! We could site the objections of Jesus Seminar scholars that we know precious little about the historical Jesus with any certainty. Indeed there is substance to all these objections. Yet, if we wish to call ourselves Christian, none of these objections can absolve us from trying to the best of our ability to discern, know, and follow Jesus the Messiah.

One of the most credible and sensitive cases for such a Christ focused norm is made by Harold Wells. He makes this case in particular for Christian theology; however, his argument is just as valid for Christian spirituality. Wells rightly points out that having a Jesus the Messiah as norm is not something we can develop deductively, but rather from within the experience of faith. He writes,

> Thus, the discipline of Christian life and thought is precisely to be disciples of Jesus Christ in everything and therefore to be centered in him. For those who confess Jesus as Lord, to depart from Christ-centeredness is to lose bearing, to fall into a kind of incoherence; it is precisely to become arbitrary in word and deed.[31]

Of course Wells is well aware of the difficulties outlined above yet he insists that it is the whole story of Jesus of Nazareth, the whole picture, "historical" and the early church's perspective from the point of view of the resurrection, all together that is our measure. This means that our following of Jesus is shaped by what we learn from the Gospels and the Bible in general. This requires study and work. It requires listening. Studying the Bible and learning what those who devote their time to researching the history and the background and the language of the Bible have to offer is important. Of course we can take it just naively; yet, part of the journey of spirituality is to move beyond a naïve faith and to find ways to study together and to learn from others. To say that "I will just read the Bible for myself and that is enough", is to deny the communal dimension of Christian spirituality and to deny the mind God has given us with which we are to love God wholly.

However, Christian spirituality is not based in a kind of academic study divorced from the Christian community. People may of course go off and study the Bible and Christian history in that way, but for us who stand within the church and wish to follow our faith in that way, Jesus the Messiah or Jesus the Christ is the norm that norms all norms. In addition we stand in community as we discern the way of Jesus Christ. Even though discerning Jesus the Messiah and his way is always difficult in every new situation, this is the task before the Christian and this is also the task for the formation of Christian leaders. Such a task never ends in its obligation to listen to the Scriptures and examine them ever afresh. It is also a task that calls us beyond human centeredness to care for the whole of creation and particularly for that part of creation where we live and breathe. God's unfolding promise through Abraham's family/Israel for the world includes not only humankind but also the reconciliation of all creation which sighs and groans in the travail of birth for the revelation of the people of God (Romans 8:22). This promise is not yet complete, there is a very important "not-yet" component as we wait for God to make us God's children and set our whole being free (Romans 8:23). It is within this tension that Christians practice the journey of spirituality.

This journey includes at it's heart care for the earth and our biosphere and it turns out, in terms of the unfolding of our understanding of God's promise through Abraham's family/Israel for the world, that it is a fundamental part of God's covenant fulfilled in Jesus the Messiah. Concern for ecological justice/righteousness is not a new fad, but built right into the understanding of God's redemption in the perspective early Christians of the first century. It is also part of the stories of identity of the ancient Hebrews.

Fostering the habits of the Spirit of Jesus the Messiah in the midst of a time in which the reign of God has come and is still coming is the task of the journey of Christian spirituality. Christian spirituality includes prayer, meditation, praise and so on, but it is never divorced from practice. To be able to practice our spirituality we must be shaped by something we can call habits. These are habits of listening to be formed into our lives on the journey.

Listening Habits – Habitus

The Latin word *habitus* is usually associated with the ancient Greek Philosopher Aristotle's concept of *hexis* when he uses *hexis* to indicate a virtue. Does our Scriptural exploration of the new perspectives on Pauline writing suggest that there are some connections between Paul's eschatological concept of the life of works of the Christian community and Aristotle's concept of *hexis* (*habitus*)? Of course we do not know if Paul studied Aristotle, we certainly have indications that he was familiar with some of the great Greek poets.[32] Nevertheless, the common concept of *habitus* derived from Aristotle's ethical concept *hexis* was well known in educated circles of the time. We do not have to turn Paul into a Greek or a Roman to argue that some of Aristotle's insight might penetrate his thinking. However, if Paul sees the development of an ethic of the Christian community how might it be similar or different from the ancient Greek process of mentoring people for *habitus*?

To answer this question we will explore Paul's approach by choosing Romans 12 which we could argue is a chapter on practicing faith and spirituality in the early Christian church. First we have to note that the thrust of Paul's thinking, when he considers the life of the Christian community, is to urge them to be transformed in a certain way. This transformation is always located in *community*. N.T. Wright argues that these pastoral comments about transformation and living in the Spirit are not practical applications of Paul's theological argument, but rather a natural and essential part of it.[33] Commentators now generally support the argument that Romans 12 and the rest of the letter is not simply an afterthought. Living out the faith practically is as important as understanding its underpinnings. We saw that for Paul in the letter to the Romans the practice of Christian life together, and the reinforcement of the covenant theme of the inclusion of both Jew and Gentile, is considered integral to the Gospel.[34] That means, that living the Gospel is part of understanding it. If we are to use Romans 12 as an example, we find several important themes for the new *habitus* of the Christian community.

The first of these is **covenant faithfulness.**

Covenant Faithfulness

First, it is clear that all Paul's exhortations for the communal life of Christian communities are rooted in his larger understanding of God's plan through Abraham's family/Israel for the whole world. The life of the Christian community is consistently, and integrally related to his theological argument that Jesus the Messiah fulfils the covenant, that all peoples are now included, and that those who believe are declared righteous because of the Messiah. This universal vision is expressed in the Christian community when it brings together the diversity of all people. Such action for unity in diversity is not an optional extra; it is the expression or the "Way of Faith" in the Messiah. Not to attend to including the diversity of peoples is to deny the covenant and to deny the work of the Messiah – such denial is akin to covenant unfaithfulness. The Christian community on the contrary is called to the **covenant faithfulness** of the inclusion of all peoples. To fulfill the covenant that we failed to keep and that Jesus has kept on our behalf we have to do the work of bringing together all people for the good of God's creation. **Covenant faithfulness** underlines the central emphasis placed in Hebrew tradition on creation as a relational reality.

This practicing **covenant faithfulness** by the loving process of bringing together all people and creation (reconciliation) requires a second habit, **eschatological living.**

Eschatological Living

As we read Romans 12 we find the ever present Pauline **eschatological** perspective. By urging the Roman Christians not to be conformed in their thinking to **"the present age"**, he implies the contrast of **"the age to come"** that has already appeared in Jesus the Messiah. The already and not yet elements of the coming reign of God thus makes up an important part of the transformative process that occurs in the life and spirituality of the Christian community. Of course this builds on the earlier emphasis in Romans 8 on active and faithful waiting as an essential part of the not yet – already tension of the eschatological time of the church. This eschatological dimension remains instructive for our own time. It means that we live not constrained by what has not yet occurred or the great disappointments we face in the now, we inhabit a world in which we live out of the possibility of what is to come and what will be. We thus live and practice our faith inspired by **eschatological living.**

By definition living and acting hopefully out of what is not yet will also require us to make sacrifices thus leading us to the next spiritual habit of **sacrificial self-giving.**

Sacrificial Self-Giving

In the opening verses of Romans 12 Paul places the transformation of the Christian community and the lives of people in it right in the story of temple sacrifice known in Second Temple Judaism. Even though the story of sacrifice remains the same, the symbols and metaphors shift. Our identity as Christians is rooted in Israel and its call for the bringing together of the nations but our Christian language gains new words. The **Christian life itself** now becomes a living and ongoing **sacrifice**. Such sacrifice reflects the mortification – giving up our lives – dimension of Christian spirituality. Transformation is not an instant event but an ongoing process in community and it involves self-giving as sacrifice. This self giving is yet again a relational self-giving. It is a living for the other. It is therefore inextricably linked to working for justice and resisting oppression and the destruction of the planet. Where people are victims of oppression their resistance and struggle for justice represents this sacrificial dimension. Sacrificial self-giving is not self-abnegation in a way that annihilates the self, but rather a giving of self in love, a love that requires being self while also committing sacrifice by opening self to others and standing for justice and peace. Such self-giving companionship in love always brings the potential and reality of suffering to the giver.

To practice the habits of covenant faithfulness, eschatological living, and sacrificial self-giving we require the habit of living out of a **transformed mind.**

Allowing a Transformed Mind

Transformation is described in Romans 12:2 as that of the **mind.** Without going into the detail exegesis of Romans 12:2 it is important to note that commentators see an appeal from Paul for a profound transformation of the whole person. Mind is not just "thinking" as in our contemporary bias, but the depths of our practical reason and moral consciousness.[35] This being said, it is clear that thinking is important. This is no proof-text for naïve anti-intellectualism or a kind of head in the sand contentless faith. Hard new rethinking is required in the habit of the transformed mind. As Karl Barth puts it,

> Neither the superficial nor legitimate protests of the anti-intellectuals are legitimate to the thinking of the thought of grace. For it is precisely the THINKING of the thought of eternity which dissolves the possibility of any adequate human thought.[36]

However, as true as the emphasis on disciplined thinking is, the "mind" here includes seeing and acting right. The verb for transformation in Romans 12:2 is rendered in the passive, translated by Douglas Moo as "be transformed". This implies that the community must *allow* the transformation that God brings to happen to them. It thus implies and opening up by sacrificial self-giving as the disposition of the Christian community in the process of forming the *habits* of Christian life. To refer to Barth again, "...– the final word of our instruction is spoken by God and Him alone; for it is He who mightily disturbs both the dogmatist and the moralist."[37] To be transformed in this way is to become mightily disturbed – Christian spirituality requires being disturbed in mind and heart to such a degree that it leads to transformative action.

These habits lead to the human response in the habit of **worship.**

Worshipping

If we read the opening two verses of Romans 12 carefully we discover that the context of the transformation of our minds is **worship.** Paul uses the word for worship that is associated with the worship of the people of Israel and their cult. This is probably to reinforce his understanding that Christian worship as a continuation of God's covenant in Jesus the Messiah. To do this he moves the temple worship symbol of the sacrifice to that of the Christian community as offering themselves as living and ongoing gifts dedicated to God. The context of transformation is worship, yet this worship is now removed from the cultic context of the temple to become the gift of the life of the community of faith that is differentiated in its unity in diversity and expands to all of life. Formation for Christian spirituality is thus to happen in the context of this wide yet radical view of worship. There is no authentic Christian spirituality without the habit of worship in ongoing self-giving openness to others in love.

This gift of ourselves includes our bodies. The Greek word for body is *soma* and we can call this valuing and giving of our physical bodies as the **somatic habit** of Christian spirituality.

Being in Body – The Somatic Habit

In Romans 12 it is not only the soul or the spirit that is presented to God, it is also the **body.** The habit of Christian life is embodied-it is somatic-in this world while living the life of the world to come. There is no priority of spirit over body here. Although we find Paul using the concept "flesh" negatively in other places representing life in rebellion against God, it is not meant to denigrate the physical body. Christian spirituality is always to be embodied. We will have resurrection bodies. The Apostle's Creed takes great pains to confess that we believe in the resurrection of the body. Our bodies are part of the creation that God redeems. This is consistent with Paul's vision of the eschatological end towards which the Christian community is on its way where all things become reconciled with and in God. These "all things" include our bodies. Creation is good. This offering of our bodies as living sacrifices in service to God is also supportive of the ecological perspective mentioned earlier in which we under-stand Christian spirituality as accountable for and in the biosphere. Worshipful embodied self-giving is the giving of service and protection of creation as out-lined in Genesis 2.

It will be clear by now that these habits of spirituality all imply effort on our side. That is why we can say Christian spirituality also requires the habit of **working hard on the way.**

Working Hard on the Way – Our Agency

Romans 12 clearly implies some **human action** on our behalf while also ex-pecting God to work right behaviour and thinking in us. Human agency here implies first **allowing** God to do this in us, but also to make and effort from our side to do so. When such and effort is made Paul ascribes it to the work of God and in some places particularly the work of the Spirit. If we go briefly to Ro-mans 8 we find this pattern expressed in the opening verses of the chapter where it is made clear that there is a "walking" or "journeying" or "way" of the Spirit that should be taken. There is an expectation that we will put to death deeds unbecoming to the Spirit (Rom 8:13), and when we make the effort to pray the Spirit comes to our aid making our prayers meaningful. The exhortations that follow in Romans 12:1-2 all imply effort on behalf of the Christian community to follow the direction in which Paul is pointing. It culminates in the final in-junction, "Do not let evil defeat you; instead, conquer evil with good." Hard work for the ethos of the reign of God is expected and required. The wonder is that where such effort is made it is a sign of God at work. Our effort is but a reflection of God's preceding and following action for us, with us, in us, and through us. This effort is well captured by the early Christian language that de-scribed faith as **a way.** The Christian life, and formation for leadership in it must also then be associated with a way or a journey – a pilgrimage – to which we are called. It is the great theme of the journey of the Christian life that we will pick up in the next chapter.

To show that this broad direction mapped out in Romans is not accidental but a major theme in Pauline writing let us briefly attend to some instructive parallels elsewhere in the Pauline writing. We have to note that Paul deals dif-ferently with the issues of the formation of Christian life in each letter; how-ever, the themes tend to reinforce each other in the light of the larger story of the fulfilment of the covenant and the eschatological location of the Christian community.

The Pauline Literature and the Habits

Galatians provides a case in point. In this letter Paul deals with the pastoral issue of Peter's behaviour but he sees it as a theological issue. Peter moves from eating with the Gentiles to withdrawing from table fellowship with them when critical leaders arrive who feel that this behaviour is wrong (see Galatians 2). Peter's behaviour becomes for Paul and example of covenant unfaithfulness. The Galatians are called to resist this unfaithfulness in the interest of including the diversity of all peoples in community-they are called to **covenant faithfulness**. Dividing Jew and Gentile again undoes the very covenant fulfilled in Jesus the Messiah. In terms of formation, here too, Paul consistently develops the **eschatological** theme in terms of active waiting (Gal 5:5) and he also emphasises the work of the Spirit in forming the Christian life. At the same time he emphasises **human agency** by referring to "planting in the field of the Spirit" (Gal 6:8), no to get tired of doing good (Gal 6:9) and urging conformity with the fruit of the Spirit as well as directing the Galatians to "let the Spirit direct their lives (Gal 5:16). The theme of **sacrifice** is engaged in terms of the command to "crucify" the old Adamic behaviour identified with "flesh" (Gal 5:24). There is thus both the expectation of concerted Christian effort to do good and right and the expectation and trust that the Spirit will work this in the lives of believers and in the community. Wright comments on the content of the word love here in Galatians,

> It is the God given Spirit driven capacity to live within the new, multiethnic family, regarding as sisters and brothers all those who share the Messiah faith.[38]

The fruit of the Spirit towards which Paul urges the Galatians are clearly **somatic** – to be fulfilled in the body and in relationship as community. Finally, although the same word for "mind" as in Romans does not appear in Galatians, Paul comments that the Spirit was sent into their "hearts", a concept of that time and culture that encapsulates both thought and feeling and therefore indicating **thinking** transformed by the Spirit. The one theme outlined above that does not appear in Galatians is worship, even though the life of the worshipping Christian community is clearly in Paul's mind as he addresses these Christians.

In the great hymn of Philippians 2 we find one of the most articulate formulations of the Gospel story[39]. In terms of the developing theme of Christian formation it is instructive that this hymn is placed as a response to a lack of unity in the community. In fact the theology of God's self-emptying incarnating action in Jesus the Messiah is exactly the ground of the author's urging for the practice of being of one accord and one mind in the Christian community (Phil 2:1-5). The covenant fulfilling Messiah came specifically to bring the bowing of **every** knee and the confessing of **every** tongue including all things in heaven and earth (Phil 2:9-10). Again, **covenant faithfulness** for the inclusion of all is at the heart of the Pauline understanding of the formation of the life of the Christian community together. Of course the letter to the Philippians contains the famous verse that urge them to work out their salvation with fear and trembling while such work is considered initiated by God (Phil 2:12-13). Here **human agency** rides on the wings of God-inspired energy. This dance between human effort and God's gracious intervention to make it possible continues throughout the letter. Consistent with other Pauline letters there is a clear **eschatological** concern, Paul uses himself as example of someone in this eschatological **journey** (race or way) towards the day of the Lord (Phil 2:16). Like Romans, Philippians clearly puts the formation of Christian community in the context of **worship**. In fact the life formed by the Spirit becomes the worship of God in the praise and glorification of God (Phil 3:3). In a most dramatic fashion the self-emptying hymn of Philippians 2 also presents the work of the Messiah as **sacrifice** in self-giving and it is this sacrificial disposition towards which Paul urges the Philippian community. Paul cites himself as an example of someone who wishes to magnify the Messiah in his body (Phil 1:20) and he likens the formation of Christians by God as a reshaping of the body (Phil 3:21). This **somatic** transformation, like the transformation of the mind in Romans is expressed as a process.

We could consistently identify all these themes in Ephesians. If the author of Ephesians is not Paul, this author clearly stays very faithful to the themes of Christian formation outlined above. We find the great covenant story affirmed in Ephesians 2 in the eloquent description of the new unity of Jew and Gentile (Eph. 2:15) and of course the call to **covenant faithfulness.** Ephesians 2:22 beautifully underlines the great focus of the Gospel on the bringing together of all peoples and building all up together as the place of God's dwelling. Here worship and the temple **worship** cult are also brought into the flow of the argument. Chapter 3 only goes on to affirm this great theme of God's fulfilled covenant at the heart of the Gospel. In the transition from Chapter 3 to 4 the dual action of God who works in the Christian community and the exhortation towards **human agency** is again raised. This human agency is walking worthily on a **way** that is placed in the context of God's call reminiscent of the covenant call of Abraham (Eph. 4:1). The renewal of the **mind** appears in Ephesians 4:23, and the putting on of the new person suggests the **somatic** quality of formation (Eph. 4:24). Chapter 5 associates the formative call to walk in the way of love according to the **sacrifice** of Christ who gave himself. The chapter continues on by re-emphasising the importance of worship and the **eschatological** tension that requires redeeming the time during these "evil days".

As we draw on this corpus of Pauline tradition a picture of the forming habits of the Christian community starts to emerge. It is not an Aristotelian mentored relationship for an aristocratic male citizen in order to gain the virtues of wisdom and citizenship; it is a formation of a community together, a community that includes all peoples, even those on the margins and specifically also gender diversity. The mentor is the Spirit, yet the Spirit requires human agency and human community in patient hope and waiting. The context is the tension between the covenant fulfilled in the Messiah and the coming Day of the Lord when all will be judged and all will be redeemed. The disposition of the community is one that calls towards covenant faithfulness in love that includes all. The life-blood of this community is expressed in a life together in sacrificial self-giving to one another which is ultimately self-giving to God in true worship, praise and glorification. Thus together on a journey this community is being transformed in mind and heart and body. We are a long way from Aristotle's habits here, but these are habits of body, mind and heart – they are habits of the reign of God.

The Synoptic Gospels and the Habits

Of course our listening to the New Testament perspectives on formation does not end with Pauline literature. By the time the Synoptic Gospels found their form certain elements of formation were clearly and strongly ensconced in early Christian communities. It may be true that many of the pastoral issues addressed in the Pauline literature do not appear as strong themes within the Gospels, yet there are also some hints that the outline developed above finds support in these later distillations of Christian teaching. The emphasis on **following** and discipleship combined with instruction underline the role of **human agency** and the transformation of the **mind**. The great judgement as presented in Matthew (25) underlines the both **somatic** and human agency elements. The **eschatological** dimension of the Synoptics is well documented, and the invitation to a **sacrificial** life in following the Christ in love and resistance is also present. The context of **worship** and prayer can also be discerned. Moreover, it can be argued that the Synoptics are a telling of the story of Jesus the Messiah as the fulfilment of **covenant** particularly in the commissioning to take the Gospel to all nations which reflects the Pauline emphasis on the inclusion of all.

As we listen to these texts and Biblical themes we discover that developing specific habits is a key part of Christian spirituality. To live out this spirituality requires **formation.**

Formation

Given these reflections on the New Testament perspectives for the formation of Christian community and Christian life, how are we to conceive formation for Christian spirituality in our present context? Are things really that different, are our challenges so far removed from the context of the Roman Empire and its challenges to the Messianic faith? Perhaps the most important response to these questions is to explore parallel challenges. Of these the challenge of inclusion of diversity is as pertinent, yet in different ways than this challenge was in the early Christian communities. For example, the question of the integration (or grafting) of the Gentile or "other" community within the early Christian-Jewish Messianic movement is no longer one that challenges us strongly. However, our post crusade, post pogrom, posts holocaust history challenges us to wrestle anew with the counter problem of the relationship of Christian communities with Judaism and gender diversity. Racism does not appear to be a large factor in these early communities, yet today we wrestle with the post-colonial history of the oppression of others by those associated with Christendom. This early communities did not have the depth of understanding of the challenges of people's experience of sexual orientation but we have to grapple with this today. Empire functions today as an oppressive force, but functions in a global financial system that operates differently and with new forms of coercion. Consumer capitalism did not exist in these early Christian communities, yet greed was also part of the human condition. A "prosperity gospel" seems absurd in those early Christian communities; today it penetrates the fastest growing Christian communities as it migrates from North American culture to cultures of the rest of the world. Massive systems of economic oppression and exploitation offer unequalled challenges to the call for redemption of the Christian Gospel. Atheism did not exist in the same way as today, after Nietzsche, protest atheism, and the death of the "Christendom god" Christians can no longer speak triumphally about God with our history of sinful appropriations of pseudo faith. When we confess that "every knee shall bow and every tongue confess", we do so in a minor tone because we know that the One to whom we bow is the self-emptying crucified One. In the light of these differences we will now reflect on formation in the light of what we read and heard so far.

The Formation of Habits

Formation for God's Covenant and our Faithful Mission on the Way

As we discovered from our exploration above, the early Christian communities were instructed that their faith was about God's plan through Abraham and his family for the whole world. All other things concerned with Christian faith fits in this big overarching story that we call the grand narrative. This means that Christian communities exist as sent into the world for this task. This means they exist in mission. We will have a final chapter to return to this theme of spirituality.

First of all, Christian communities exist within the first and fundamental mission of God's act of creation and second they exist in the redemptive mission of God for the whole of humankind and all creation. The most basic dimension of formation for Christian spirituality is to understand and embrace this essential missionary nature of Christian community. This means that one understands and embraces one's call to have a role in God's mission towards all peoples and all creation. God's plan, or the story that explains the meaning of the existence of creation, is expressed in terms of the covenant that is also a promise to each of us. This promise and God's unique way of fulfilling the promise in Jesus the Messiah, is what Paul refers to as the secret plan now revealed, or the *mystery* (this word mystery was translated sacrament in Latin). As those who are being formed for Christian spirituality we are drawn into this mystery and thus fed by the "sacrament"/mystery of Jesus the Messiah. This sacramental dimension of covenant faithfulness will be explored further under the themes of sacrifice and worship. We will also devote a chapter to this later.

As we are being formed for Christian spirituality we need to hear this story, repeat and memorise it, learn it by heart, and live out of it as our stance in life. The followers of Judaism repeat something they call the *shema*. It is a reminder of the central belief in the unity of God. The *shema* of formation for spirituality is not just the constant reminder "Hear O Israel the Lord your God is One", but expanded to,

> "Hear all peoples your God is self-giving and faithful to God's promise to redeem all things through God's Messiah and in Him through you all people and all creation."

We can describe this story metaphorically as the Christian Song of the Universe, a song in which we are all called to join in harmony. As we form and are formed for Christian spirituality we are called to learn and sing this song in all dimensions of life. Our hearts and voices, our poetry and prayers, our loving and giving, is to be penetrated by this great song. If this happens we will be living in **faithfulness.**

Formation for Faithfulness

A major part of formation for Christian spirituality is to grasp and embrace our faithful response to God's promise in the mystery of Jesus the Messiah. In the Protestant tradition our emphasis on justification by faith has led us to an understanding of faith that was often self-focused. It became uniquely concerned with how my faith in God brings me to a place of justification. Recent studies of Paul in his context, explored above, challenge this self-absorbed attitude. Justification is indeed an act in which God declares us justified, but it fits in the wider context of the covenant in which we are now included. This covenant is not focused on us first, but on God's redemptive purpose for all peoples and all things. Abraham's faithfulness, despite his struggles and doubts, was fed from the well of God's promise that he would become a blessing to all families of the earth. Formation for Christian spirituality is fed from the same well of promise and hope for the other not just for the self. It is not a matter of removing the comfort of faith and trust in God's faithful judgement on us as individuals, but it is a matter of linking this comfort with a mission towards others, a journey that cannot divorce our own comfort and joy in faith from God's intention to bring well-being to all. Formation for Christian spirituality requires a recasting of our faith in the mould of faithfulness for others and ultimately for all creation. Where we engage the task of formation our example and our ritual need to be fed from a constant focus on the "liturgy of the other" to the point that this liturgy becomes our life theme. By using the expression "liturgy of the other" we are saying that meeting others as people or the otherness of the rest of creation is a kind of worship space. The Lithuanian philosopher, Emmanuel Levinas, expressed this in terms of the Rabbinic wisdom in the proverb, "My neighbour's physical need is my spiritual need[40]."

When we live our lives in a constant liturgy of the other we will of necessity **engage diversity.**

Formation for the Engagement of Diversity

Covenant faithfulness and encountering the other bring us to an understanding that the Christian community is about the extension of God's blessing to all families of the earth, or, in the words of Matthew, all nations. It is of course no accident that Genesis 12 follows on Genesis 11 that tells the story of the Tower of Babel and the fragmentation of humankind in different tongues and cultures. The unfolding Genesis narrative almost immediately responds with God's redemptive purpose in contrast to the human hubris. God's plan through Abraham's family for the world is to bring all families back into God's redemptive domain of blessing. It is for this reason that Paul remains concerned with the bringing together of diversity in the Christian community and this is why he consistently describes the place and the role of faith and the Christian community as the place where there is no longer separation. In this community there is diversity, but this diversity finds its redemption in the unity brought by the Messiah. It is clear that Paul's argument is not to forcefully harmonize different kinds of people into a unity without diversity. Rather, the Jerusalem Council as described in Acts 15 determines that the "gentiles should not be troubled", that is, they should maintain there identity and difference. The requirements placed on different peoples do not go to their cultural identity, gender, or station in life, but rather to a concern for honouring God. This, in the mind of the Jerusalem Council means not engaging in behaviour that seems to support Roman cultic religion, and to behave in ways that are faithful to a community of covenant and commitment by abstaining from community destroying sexual practice. It must be noted that this prohibition was not a denigration of sexuality and bodily existence. In fact sexually is valued and placed within the context of faithful relationship and community. Formation for Christian spirituality requires exposure to and an evolving understanding of unity in diversity. This means recognising, respecting, and cherishing the other in their otherness. It requires the inclusion of people without attempting to wipe out their difference. We are called to be community in diversity and we are to be formed in that way.

By living in a diversity-affirming community the Christian community and its spirituality lives in **eschatological hope.**

Formation for Eschatological-Hopeful Living

We have already encountered the habit of eschatological living in Romans 12. The contrast between the present age and the age to come, the already and the not yet, and the questions and struggles implied by this dimension presents another key aspect of formation for Christian spirituality. Christian leaders are constantly faced with the dissonance between faith and hope and the experience of the present age. The habit of active faithful waiting that the Bible calls hope is the response of covenant faithfulness. In our earlier exploration of Paul's letters we have noted the importance that the Spirit plays for Paul in this regard. It is in the travailing and comforting and goading presence of the Spirit that we are able to be hopeful in what appears to be a hopeless and doomed world. It is in the Spirit that we are able to be hopeful even in the face of our own unfaithfulness. It is after all the Great Spirit – the *Ruah* of God – that is described as hovering over the chaos of unformed creation... Is it possible to actively form a habit of hope?

Does the injunction to be hopeful make any sense, or does it imply picking ourselves up by our own bootlaces? The direction taken in Pauline letters draws us to another alternative. Here active waiting is both an effort on our side and a gift of the presence of the Spirit from God. Most of all, it is relational practice. It is in the "not yet" that we are able to demonstrate love in the face of fear, hopelessness and suffering. To be formed for Christian spirituality is to grasp this creative tension between our action and God's gift. There are many biblical narratives that demonstrate the delicate balance between action and gift. Earlier we have explored Abraham's sacramental discovery of the sign of the many stars in the sky. Then there are the priests marching into the Jordan and only when their feet touch the water does it part (Josh 3:15-16) and so on. There is a connection between mystery/sacrament-sign and the combination of active waiting and gift from God. In formation for Christian spirituality this sacramental connection linked to active waiting is a habit to be inculcated.

Living in eschatological hope enables us to be formed to live **sacrificially.**

Formation for Sacrificial Living

The move in Romans 12:1-2 from cultic language of sacrifice to the gift of the Christian life as a sacrifice that we encountered when we looked at the habit of living in **self-giving sacrifice** is of prime importance to formation for Christian spirituality. It was John Calvin that argued that the sacrifice that is appropriate in the sacramental setting of the church is the sacrifice of the gift of oneself to God in worship,

> Under the other kind of sacrifice, which we have called eucharistic, are included all the offices of charity, by which, while we embrace our brethren, we honour the Lord himself in his members; in fine, all our prayers, praises, thanksgivings, and every act of worship which we perform to God. *All these depend on the greater sacrifice with which we dedicate ourselves, soul and body, to be a holy temple to the Lord.* [41]

Let us note the embodied quality of this understanding of Eucharistic sacrament and sacrifice. In fact, Calvin begins with acts of charity, speak then of the embracing our "brethren" (the diversity of fellow believers). Moreover the city of Geneva in his time was a refugee city filled with religious refugees from many different cultures. Caring for these refugees becomes for Calvin a matter of sacramental faithfulness. In fact, he points out that by honouring others we honour God. Sacrifice here becomes an embodied self-giving with social and spiritual ramifications and inextricably linked to loving others. It is this kind of sacrifice that informs our understanding of some of the essential habits to be formed in Christian leaders. Far from being an other-worldly spirituality, this implies a socially engaged political spirituality strengthened by the context of cultic worship in community. We also need to note that Roman 12:1-2 describes this self-giving as a process, and we shall later see that we can also relate this to a journey. Self-giving is not a once and for all act, it is a disposition, a habit, of action for every day of one's life that is in essence an expression of love.

Living in self-giving sacrifice places us in a disposition that will allow our **minds to be transformed.**

Formation for a Transformed Mind

At first blush the reference made earlier to Karl Barth's commentary on the Romans seem to imply that the transformed mind is a kind of intellectual process. While the intellectual is rightly important as Barth points out, it is clear that the mind in Romans calls us to a moral consciousness and a practiced reasonability. David Bosch described this as expanded rationality[42]. This rationality is not mindless action, but neither is it actionless thought. To be transformed in the mind is to bring together our experience and the observation of the sighing and suffering of people and creation with disciplined thought and thoughtful action. People who have wrestled with Christian faith and the suffering of the poor have long argued that one should always start with solidarity with the poor and suffering and that analysis, biblical reflection and critical engagement follows from this process. There is much truth in this emphasis, particularly if the decision to be in solidarity with the most vulnerable in the world proceeds from experience and thought integrated with the challenge of the Messianic self-giving and solidarity of Jesus himself.

The cloth of such theological action and reflection is not a circle or a spiral, but a complex and interwoven pattern of warp, woof, circle and spiral brought together in a constant process of transformation. Christian spirituality lives in such a dynamic ongoing dance. Perhaps, rather than abstract images, what we need to grasp is that this is a kind of *poetry* that engages mind and heart, action and reflection alike? We are not transformed by simply reading words on a page; we are transformed when our lives are addressed in its completeness with seeing, hearing, feeling, smelling and tasting. Often the transformative turning points of our lives (our conversions) occur when we are confronted to see and are then drawn in by such seeing and the empathising that arises out of it into solidarity in action. Transformation of the mind is to see clearly and to see what others do not necessarily see. It is to see differently, to see with the eyes of the world to come, rather than with the eyes of this present age. How do we form such habits of seeing? Of course, such seeing is a gift, but it is also a function of being there with others. Formation for a transformed mind thus challenges us to expose others and ourselves to the suffering and godlessness of the world. In the words of Karl Barth cited earlier, it is to be "mightily disturbed in mind and heart".

Formation for transformation in engagement with the suffering and god-lessness of the world occurs within the framework of **worship.**

Formation for Worshipful Living

It is striking in Romans 12:1 to find how wide the idea of "reasonable worship" is. Even though Paul uses the cultic word he invites the Christian community in Rome to give themselves bodily to God and in these total self-giving they offer worship. Worship is therefore the beginning and end of Christian service in the embodied and ongoing process of self-giving. Theologians call this **doxology.** Again we are forced to ask ourselves if it is indeed possible to form others and ourselves for such a habit of self-giving worship? But as we read Romans 12 it becomes clear that we are again back at the creative tension between offering ourselves – our work – and allowing ourselves to be transformed – the work of the Spirit. In the traditions of formation for Christian spirituality participating in and leading Christian worship has always played a pivotal role. Just think of the many moments of worship, reading and singing of the Psalms and prayer in the Rule of Saint Benedict. This practice of worship remains as important today, yet it needs to be clear in our formation that we draw on a much deep-er theology, a theology of self-giving, when we participate in and lead formal or public worship in community. Moreover, we draw on a theology that un-derstands worship as the giving of self in all dimensions of life as an ongoing process of love.

Worship for us requires the brain, vocal cords, and heart of a human being – it happens in the body – we are thus to be formed to live our faith in **living bodies.**

Formation for Living in our Bodies

Several times in our discussion above the embodied nature of Christian life has been highlighted. It is clear that Paul's vision of redemption is one that includes all dimensions of creation and one that values physical existence. We have noted that this touches on a spirituality that is embodied. "Flesh" in conflict with "Spirit" has often been wrongly and harmfully interpreted in Christian tradition to be about the physical body that passes away over against the spirit that is eternal. Perhaps we see the first signs of this in the early desert ascetics. In contrast, Paul takes the body very seriously. He writes of disciplining his body and bearing suffering that fills the suffering of Christ in it. This body, although it may, like all parts of our human condition lead us astray, is to be given, and used for the glory of God. The habit of embodied and disciplined life in body is one that connects with the larger dimension of the physical creation and its redemption. Even though, surely, Paul had no sense of the environmental catastrophe we are presently bringing upon ourselves on the planet, his vision of creation suffering and groaning and sighing for redemption through the revelation of God's people is one that affirms our present awareness of human responsibility for creation. It leads us right back to the covenant of creation that calls us to tend and care for the created world around us. We need no stronger argument for embodied formation than the resurrected body of Jesus Christ as described in the Gospels. In these stories Christ is not a ghost, his transformed existence is in body. Thus our vocation is also to live in body. Formation for Christian spirituality thus requires the building of awareness of our embodied place in the biosphere and our responsibility for it.

When we take our bodies and the physical world seriously then we are challenged to **work hard for the reign of God and its justice** that is to come.

Formation for Working Hard with the Reign of God

The discussion above has repeatedly raised the tension between human agency and God's activity in for and through us. Our exploration of the work of N.T. Wright has shown that setting these two dimensions in contrast to one another is misleading, particularly as we explore Pauline literature. The traditional Protestant preoccupation with "grace" as opposed to "works" leads us astray. Even the Calvinistic emphasis on works as acts of thankfulness in response to God's grace, though helpful, may still create a quietism that does not reflect the way Paul sees the integration of the gracious work of the Spirit with our own effort do act justly, to love mercy and to walk humbly with God. For Paul there is no dichotomy, where works of love and redemptive action are displayed it witnesses to the work of the Spirit that wills and works in us. As we exert ourselves the best we can to do God's work and to live in God's reign we discover the gracious presence of the Spirit that makes it possible. We do not sit back and wait for things to happen, we act and when we act it becomes a gift of the Spirit. For this reason the Pauline corpus as well as the synoptic Gospels are filled with instructions for living and injunctions. Even the final judgement, we gather from Matthew 25, will be based on our acts of solidarity with the most vulnerable in society. Our main text for reflection here, Romans 12 follows the giving of self as living sacrifice and the command to be transformed and renewed in mind with a series of instructions about how to use our differing gifts in Christian community for the benefit of all. As we are formed for Christian spirituality and as we form others these injunctions to find a diversity of gifts and to exercise them for the good of the whole, provide a platform for ongoing formative action. Above all, it means that we will challenge one another to act while taking care to recognise the gracious work of the Spirit when our action bears fruit.

These insights raise the encouragement of spiritual disciplines as an important and valid part of the process of formation for Christian spirituality. The Christian worship practices of prayer, praise, study, confession, giving, sharing, and acting in solidarity are practices to which those formed should be consistently exposed. As they act in these practices they are to discover the work of the Spirit. These reflections on human agency take us back to the ancient rule of Saint Benedict.

Reformation critiques of monastic life were aimed at particular abuses at the time. It also emphasised the responsibility of all people of faith to live within the spiritual disciplines. In addition, it emphasised that grace precedes every human action. Rather than believing that one follows the rule and God's blessing will follow, the reformers claimed that God's blessing and grace comes and one follows the rule in response. Recent Pauline scholarship has brought these positions closer together by allowing us to understand that the following of the rule can be born out of the grace of God even as we exert ourselves to follow it. Later we will see that even the monastic disciplines, and particularly the Benedictine rule clearly emphasised that all action and all obedience arises first out of the grace of God that precedes all.

How then can the Rule of Saint Benedict help to form such action in the grace of the Spirit in us? Is this medieval Christian tradition not completely out of touch with the contemporary hyper reality of our consumer-capitalist, technologically obsessed world? What I propose here is not that we should be formed for spirituality in modern monasteries, although that might not be a bad option for some, but rather that we draw on the profound monastic tradition as we form people for spirituality. Such spirituality for our time and future that goes against the tide of our current age requires extraordinary tenacity and an ability to persist when it seems all is lost. This is exactly what the medieval monastic tradition did and what tapping into its spirituality has to offer us. David Bosch put it this way,

> I am referring to the monks' patience, tenacity, and perseverance. Wave after wave of invasion swept over Europe, as one warlike barbarian people after the other gained the upper hand. Saracens, Huns, Lombards, Tartars, Saxons, Danes – all of these attacked the unsuspecting peasants and destroyed the monasteries. But monasticism possessed extraordinary resilience and recuperative power. [43]

Nothing less than a spirituality of the long haul would do in the face of our contemporary challenges as Christian communities. Such spirituality was exemplified and deeply embedded in the lives of monks and nuns in the Benedictine tradition. It involves being formed and allowing us to be formed in the spiritual habits outlined in Romans 12.

Saint Benedict offered a practical and moderate rule that relied on the common sense of a life embodied in this world but living for the world to come. Over centuries it proved to be indestructible, resilient, wise, and faithful to the Gospel call. Without being intentionally missionary it carried a missional dimension in its basic makeup that would constantly overcome impossible challenges. Today the explicit Benedictine movement is still alive and well, and still at the heart of most Western spirituality, however, what I advocate here is an implicit cultivated Benedictine spirituality in the process of formation of Christians. Perhaps not all the elements of the Rule are equally helpful, but it remains a remarkable and inspiring document even today.

Much of Benedict's original rule deals with practical instructions for specific spiritual disciplines at different times in the Christian year. Without necessarily following these exactly, these instructions emphasise a spirituality that is deeply rooted in the disciplines of prayer, the reading of the psalms, other readings from the Bible, and singing. This is symbolised by *ora* (prayer). The work of the monk is rooted in these disciplines while also drawing on Benedict's instructions for a particular disposition of humility, reverence in prayer, singular focus on God, patience and keeping an even temper. Over time Benedictine monasteries also became repositories of knowledge research, the copying of texts, and study. Monks are also instructed to engage the world in physical labour, gardening, cooking and cleaning up. These aspects of the Rule can be symbolised by *labora* (work). Of course, these dispositions reflect the fruit of the Spirit we have referred to earlier, and also signal that this is a spirituality of community. Thus the rhythm of Benedictine spirituality remains the balance between prayer and work – *ora et labora*. It also stipulates simplicity of living for the monk and a sense of complete equality within the community no matter what station in life one comes from. The Benedictine way also became associated with caring for the sick and hospitality.

It is easy to see how these elements of spirituality merge with our earlier reflection on biblical material. In fact, we can argue that it embodies all the elements of Paul's theology discussed above. Its equality in the midst of diversity stresses covenant faithfulness, it engages the world around it with practical work and care while it lives eschatologically out of the power of the world to come, it calls the monks to sacrificial self-giving love, and to a study of the Bible and recitation of the Psalms that is mind transforming, it places all in the context of worship in the great rule, *Ut in omnibus glorificetur Deus* (that in all things God may be glorified). All these actions are practical and embodied by all the monks do, and of course the very existence of the Rule and commitment to it in vow and community suggests human agency that is borne by God's presence in the Spirit.

Later, in Chapter 4, we will explore the sacramental nature of the spirituality of formation as we explore the habits of the coming reign of God that feed our action towards the love of others, the nations and the cosmos. These habits can be captured by the basic Benedictine movements of prayer and work, but must be unpacked in greater detail. Benedictine spirituality, thus imagined, is walking a way – it is a deeply committed journey. Out next chapter will take us further into reflection on the importance of formation as journey. To be formed for Christian spirituality in our time is to be rooted in this kind of spirituality with discipline and commitment to community.

Conclusion

We have learned in this chapter that we are not simply called, but that our call requires us to listen for the meaning of the call and to discern the content of the call. In this process of listening we have found themes arising out of the Scriptural text and enforced by Christian monastic tradition that invites those called to particular habits or disciplines. We have discovered that this requires effort on our behalf, effort that will prove to draw its origin and strength in the Spirit of God when we make it. We have heard that we are called in Christian community to go on a journey of habit and discipline. It is this journey we shall explore next.

Notes

1. Wright, N.T. *Justification* Downers Grove: Intervarsity Press, 2009, 95.

2. Batter my heart, three person'd God; for, you As yet but knocke, breathe, shine, and seeke to mend; That I may rise, and stand, o'erthrow mee,'and bend Your force, to breake, blowe, burn and make me new. I, like an usurpt towne, to'another due, Labour to'admit you, but Oh, to no end, Reason your viceroy in mee, mee should defend, But is captiv'd, and proves weake or untrue. Yet dearely'I love you,'and would be loved faine, But am betroth'd unto your enemie: Divorce mee,'untie, or breake that knot againe; Take mee to you, imprison mee, for I Except you'enthrall mee, never shall be free, Nor ever chast, except you ravish mee.(John Donne 1572-1631)

3. Breuggemann, W. *Genesis: Interpretation - A Bible Commentary for Teaching and Preaching.* Atlanta: John Knox Press, 1982, 116.

4. Ibid., 117.

5. See Lev 26:12 and Deut 23:15 as examples of a Biblical use of this metaphor.

6. In the Hebrew language this sentence also means that the goodness of creation is expressed in the way it functions correctly or rightly.

7. Karl Barth rightly points out that Jesus is the man for his fellow human beings, but my argument is here that he is also more than that, he is the man for the redemption of all creation. See Barth, K. *Church Dogmatics III: The Doctrine of Creation 2.* Edinburgh: T & T Clark, 1960, 211.

8. Mark 8:35 see also Breuggemann, Ibid., 118.

9. Ibid., 118, & see also Wenham discussion of the contrast between those who "disdain" Abram in relation to the stronger language of the "curse" of God, Wenham, Ibid., 276.

10. Breuggemann, Ibid., 119.

11. Wenham, G.J. *Word Biblical Commentary. Genesis 1-15.* Nashville: Thomas Nelson, 1987, 278.

12. Sailhamer, J.H. *The Pentateuch as Narrative:A Biblical-Theological Commentary.* Grand Rapids: Zondervan, 1992, 139.

13. See Breuggemann, Ibid., 140 and Wenham's helpful discussion of the genesis of this chapter, particularly the source criticism and the question if it draws on deuteronomic tradition or vice versa. Wenham, Ibid., 326.

14. Ibid., 333.

15. Breuggemann, Ibid., 50.

16. Wenham's translation, Ibid., 324.

17. Ibid., 329.

18. Breuggemann, Ibid., 145.

19. Ibid., 330.

20. I am relying on Wright's work here as my primary source, however, it is important to note that Wright stands is a tradition of Pauline scholarship that has consistently and convincingly argued for the thorough Judaistic character of Paul's thought rather than the argument earlier in the twentieth century that Paul had to be understood as a Hellenistic thinker. In this Wright works out of the premises developed by E.P. Sanders see for example, Sanders, E.P. *Paul and Palestinian Judaism: A Comparison of Patterns of Religion.* London: SCM, 1977 & Sanders, E.P. *Paul: A very short introduction.* Oxford University Press, 2001.

21. Of course it was Karl Barth who argued that Jesus Christ is really the only sacrament of God. See, Barth K. *Church Dogmatics. The Doctrine of Reconciliation IV2.* Edinburgh: T & T Clark, 1996, 55.

22. Bonhoeffer, D. *The Cost of Discipleship.*

23. Rom 8:22 Good News Bible.

24. See Moltmann's sensitive treatment of the questions of protest atheism in, Moltmann, J. *The Crucified God.* Minneapolis: Fortress Press, 1993, 219-227.

25. Wright, Ibid., 250.

26. Ibid., 239.

27. Ibid., 188.

28. Ibid., 75. and for a discussion of this idea in Paul with regards to Philippians 144-145. See also the work of Sanders cited above.

29. See Wright's detailed discussion of this idea, Ibid., 182ff.

30. Ibid., 240ff. See also, Wright, N.T. *Paul for Everyone: Romans: Part II: Chapters 9-16* Louisville: Westminster, John Knox, 2004, 24 ff.

31. Wells, H. *The Christic Center: Life-Giving and Liberating* New York: Orbis Books, 2004, 118-119. See Wells' complete argument throughout the whole of Chapter 4 of his book.

32. For example the Book of Acts report Paul quoting from the Greek poets Epimenides and Aratus.

33. Wright, *Paul for Everyone*, Ibid., 72.

34. In addition to Wright's comments cited above, Douglas Moo describes this passage as playing a pivotal role in the whole letter to the Romans. Moo, D.J. *The Epistle to the Romans* Grand Rapids: Eerdmans, 1996, 745-748.

35. Moo, Ibid., 756.

36. Barth, K. *The Epistle to the Romans* Oxford: Oxford University Press, 1968, 438.

37. Ibid., 438.

38. Wright, *Justification* Ibid., 139.

39. Of course, there are many scholars who believe that Paul quotes an early Christian hymn here that perhaps does not originate with him.

40. Critchley, Simon & Bernasconi, Robert (Eds.) *The Cambridge Companion to Levinas.* Cambridge: Cambridge University Press, 2002, 107.

41. Calvin, J. *The Institutes of the Christian Religion. Book IV.* Chapter 18:16. Translated by H. Beverage Grand Rapids: Eerdmans, 1957, 2618.

42. Bosch D.J. *Transforming Mission: Paradigm Shifts in Theology of Mission.* New York: Orbis, 1991, 352-355

43. Ibid., 232-233.

3

Journey

These fragments of stone and story, these traces of fragile testimony, still resist—as they have resisted for centuries—the triumphalism of ecclesiastical empire. Hideouts, off the beaten track, without foundation. Cut against the grain. Self-effacing, modest, vulnerable, welcoming. Sanctuaries for migrants. Shelters for the exiled. Footholds for the forgotten. Arks. Perfect places for rejected personas to come and lay their heads. Ciphers, perhaps, of a transfiguring God.[1]

Thus writes the philosopher Richard Kearny about his pilgrimage to the holy places of Nazareth, Capernaum, and Tabha. In his philosophical reflection on the Gospel story of the transfiguration on the mount Kearney concludes that the enigma of the transfiguration reminds us that we are embodied creatures in space and time who need our pilgrimages to sacred places. In short, what Kearney suggests can be described as our need for sacrament. Whether we think of the sacrament of the awe inspiring expanse of stars at night that gave Abraham comfort, or we think of the bread and wine in the Christian community, or the sacramental presence of a neighbour in friendship and mutual care, we remain always creatures who need to embody and experience meaning and faith in space and time. We need something or someone who can be seen to embody the promise we cannot see. Like Abraham on his journey to the Promised Land or like the disciples on the journey to Jerusalem with Jesus the visible signs of God's promise come on the journey. Christian spirituality is a lived, expressed, experienced and thought out on the way. It is a journey. On this journey we are shaped for life with God even as we live and move and breathe in God.

In the next chapter we will focus more specifically on sacrament and community as they appear on this journey. In this chapter we will touch on these two dimensions as well because they are both vital parts of the journey of Christian spirituality. We can say that the journey we are now to explore can be summarised by the two great Biblical commandments, first to love God and then our neighbour as ourselves. This suggests that the journey of Christian spirituality always involves moving to a deeper love of God and at the same time moving to a deeper love of our neighbours, people and creation. But this love is a journey and is expressed in action, movement, and relationship. This journey is a function and a necessity of the "not yet" reality we live in with all its pain and suffering, yet it is also the gift of being able to realise a free and loving life with God and neighbour. It sounds so simple and it is! However, it is not an easy journey.

Because this journey is so challenging the ancient Christian tradition spoke of it as a pilgrimage captured in the Latin expression *perigrinatio pro Christi.*

Journey – Pilgrimage

The monastic ideal of pilgrimage for the sake of Christ (*perigrinatio pro Christi*) is one that can be traced back to the Celtic wanderers perhaps most powerfully symbolised by Columba (521-597) who founded his monastery on the Island of Iona and sent monks to share the Gospel with the Picts on the Scottish mainland.[2] These wandering monks travelled into Northern Europe by the end of the sixth century, and were soon followed by women in vocation in a monastery founded by Burgundofara (643-655). Yet, these early medieval examples from the Celts built on stories of early wanderings recorded in the Scriptures in the book of Acts as with the journeys of Saint Paul, Barnabas, Peter and others. In addition, the early Christian document, *Didache* records the common practice of wandering evangelists.[3]

Even though these examples speak of physical travel for the sake of the Gospel, they were never divorced from the objective of the journey towards holiness for the traveller and towards the hearts of those with whom such travelling Christians engaged in different parts of the world. In fact there is something fundamentally journey-like in Christian faith. Thus, Daniel von Allmen has argued that we find a theme in the Book of Acts that supports the idea that the blessing of the Holy Spirit went with the adventurous travelling Christians who crossed new boundaries with the Gospel, rather than with the conservers who wished to keep the Gospel the way they knew it in a way that held it for themselves only and for their own edification.[4] The freshness of new engagement and dynamic of building new relationships as well as reaching out to new peoples clearly represent a strong theme already present in the New Testament. The Gospels tell the story of Jesus in terms of a journey to Jerusalem and the cross. We can of course trace the importance of spiritual journey right to the Old Testament in the epic journey of Abraham from his native land to the promised one, in the journey of Jacob to find a wife, the journey of Josef to Egypt, the journey of the people through the desert and the so on. Most fundamentally we find the journey motif in Adam and Eve as they journey away from hiding, isolation, and blame towards the call of God back to love. In all these cases the physical journey was accompanied by a journey of faith, a journey to the neighbour and a journey to and with God.

The metaphor of the journey also has important implications in the light of our exploration of the themes and habits of the formation of Christian community that we explored in the last chapter. The journey to the nations and the world speaks of covenant faithfulness to God's promise to bring blessings to all nations and to welcome diversity in unity. The necessary move to the unknown that every journey involves, speaks of the eschatology of hope – being sojourners in this world rather than completely at home. To use the words of *Lumen Gentium* 6 from the Second Vatican Council, "The Church, while on earth it journeys in a foreign land away from the Lord, is life an exile [sic]."

There is therefore a sense in which we are not of "this age" as we journey towards the "age to come". The journey of Christian spirituality therefore is one that is always in some sense homeless while travelling, working and hoping for the home that we are promised. This dimension of sojourning and, to a certain degree homelessness, also speaks to the theme of sacrifice. As with Abraham who journeyed away from his land of birth and family, so we leave behind important securities on the journey of faith. Most of all, all faith journeys require a leaving behind of our own self-reliance and human hubris. In the New Testament, and particularly in the Gospels, this idea of turning away from our previous life and self-reliance to a new journey in following Jesus the Messiah is described by the concept repentance that simply means to turn in a new direction. We can thus say that Abraham's epic journey in which he moves away from his people and all that is familiar to him to the new place where God calls and leads him is one of the great demonstrations of the concept of repentance. It is, to refer back to the reflections on Abraham's blessings in the previous chapter, a negation that precedes the blessing of God that returns all to us. Or to use the sacrificial language of 1 Peter, "I appeal to you, my friends, as strangers and refugees in this world! Do not give in to bodily passions, which are always at war against the soul."[5] Texts like these are often attenuated by Christians to represent little personal temptations in their lives, however, the bodily passions referred to here are the things that divert us from the journey towards love of God, neighbour and creation. It is about moving from the superficial passions to the deep passion of opening ourselves to God and one another. We will see later in this chapter how the theme of transformation can be intimately linked to the ongoing empassioned act of journey that is also an ongoing process of repentance.

By now it should become clear that we are formed on this journey for and by the habits described in the previous chapter. This would be a good time to remind ourselves what they are. They include the habits of **covenant faithfulness, eschatological living, sacrificial self-giving, transformed mind, worship, somatic living,** and **working hard on the way.** This is how we engage the journey of Christian spirituality. But, we cannot do so if we are not rooted in a profound understanding of who we are. We need identity. It is not identity as a static thing but identity that is being shaped, changed, and transformed on a journey of love. We need to be secure in being able to say, "This is who I am as a Christian who journeys with these habits as my structure and strength."

To clarify our identity we will draw on two important thinkers of the 20th century, Karl Barth and Paul Tillich.

Towards Identity on the Journey

I will argue here that the theologies of Paul Tillich (1886–1965) and Karl Barth (1886–1968), although in fundamental ways different, are helpful to clarify who we are on the journey. The concept of identity is described in theology by the word "anthropology". "Theological anthropology" is really the theory of who we are. Barth helps us to understand just how integrally "who we are" is tied to the Man Jesus the Messiah. Tillich helps us to understand how important it is to engage the journey to enable us to be who we are to be and to become who we are to become. Tillich speaks of this as "the courage to be" in the face of anxiety, fear and meaninglessness. This courage to be is accomplished by engaging the world. As we do so we are transformed. This transformation involves being as ourselves and being with others in community. The call to be on this journey of constant turning and following is the truth of our existence and part of our destiny within the covenant call of God. It will become clear here that engaging the journey in this way shapes us with the habits of Christian spirituality – covenant faithfulness, self-giving sacrifice, being transformed in mind, and living in our bodies.

As it was on the journey of Abraham where he heard the promises of God, and as it was on the journey and in a sacred or thin place[6] that Jacob saw the great ladder ascending to heaven, so it is with us. Our worship grows as a function of our journey. We may be stuck, wrestle with the dark night of the soul (anxiety, guilt, self-loathing, meaninglessness), or find ourselves completely bereft of hope, yet all these conditions invite us on a journey to worship. Even the weekly rhythms of worship involve journeys, walks, drives, and movement towards community where worship occurs. Whether we talk about the journey of a short walk down the street, a long pilgrimage to a place of worship, or the journey of discovering how God's love is manifest in our neighbour, worship and journey are interrelated in basic ways. Even the liturgy of public worship can be described as a journey that visits the stations of call, listening, responding, prayer and praise, sacrament and sending. All these things occur in our bodies. They require the movement of our limbs, the use of eyes, mouth, ears and nose, and the raising of our voices. Thus we are shaped into the habit of worship.

Such journeys might be unusually short. We can think of Dietrich Bonhoeffer's striking journey in prison during World War II. Locked in a cell, with barely the possibility of movement, he penned his letters from prison that would cast its theological influence right into the twenty first century. This journey described in those letters ended in the journey to the gallows. Yet, whether long or short, a journey is always embodied – somatic. Finally, there will be no journey if we do not move, if we do not respond, if we do not turn, if we do not act with our human agency. The most destructive "bodily passions" are those that keep us stationary in frantic activity towards self-indulgence without engaging loving relationships. Likewise, there is not spiritual journey where looking back does not allow us to see that it is God who moved us in the first place.

From this reflection it is clear that journey is a key part of the Christian life, and an essential part of the formation for Christian spirituality. There can be no formation without journey. How then do we journey in formation for spirituality and how are we to invite others on the journey?

The Journey of the Neighbour

It was a very short journey that launched me on a path that I would never escape. She invited me. She was a middle aged black woman who cleaned my university residence room in Cape Town, South Africa. I was 18 years old and had just "awakened" to the reality of the oppressive apartheid regime and its frightening power. I realised that she was a neighbour, a person with dignity, a family, sorrows and joys, and I asked her about it one morning when I skipped class. I was not ready for the enthusiasm with which she shared her story with me. I learned more than I bargained for and before I knew it I was invited to the township where her teenage son would act in a play. For a white South African boy the journey to the black township (a separate place where the apartheid government forced black people to stay under appalling conditions) was relatively short by car but daunting in its cloud of uncertainties and fear. That Saturday night I made the journey. I found myself the total stranger – the other – in the midst of a people and a culture I barely knew, even though we lived 20 minutes away all my life. One white boy among several hundred black people I was welcomed like a celebrity and felt an odd shame about having such a fuss made over such a small gesture of travel and common humanity. I sat in the middle of the hall an enjoyed the jokes that sometimes skirted dangerously close to being crude even for a Monty Python fan like I. When it was all over my newfound friend and neighbour's son came and stood next to me. He took my hand and held it tight. It was an act of courage for him. In apartheid South Africa black and white did not often touch each other in this way. He had tears in his eyes when he said "thank you." Then he said, "Please don't judge my people for their crude jokes, they are not all like this…" It was I who was deeply ashamed at that moment. It was the beginning of a transformation. Some weeks later my friend did no longer come and clean my room. When I enquired I was told that she had disappeared. Perhaps, mused the residence manager, she was sent back to the Transkei, there must have been something wrong with her pass that allowed her to work here…?

It is my experience that every process of transformation, big or small, in my life begins with meeting the other as my neighbour. It was so with my friend on this occasion and it would be so many other times in my life. Could I ever objectify people with a different skin colour as a "they" after this journey into the township? Of course not, when one's conscience is raised, it is hard to escape its ongoing goading. Could I look at the political system in my country of the time in the same way? Of course not,! Something in me was transformed. So dramatic was the transformation that it seemed that the prophets of the Old Testament spoke straight to me and to the political situation in my country. Surely, the Prophet Isaiah was speaking to us when he said, "I will bring you gold instead of bronze, Silver and bronze instead of iron and wood, and iron instead of stone. Your rulers will no longer oppress you; I will make them rule with justice and peace"?[7] The Prophet Amos took on a new contemporary quality in my eyes, I became angry, incensed, politicised. I discovered the righteous anger of Jesus of whom I was taught in Sunday school to say "Gentle Jesus Meek and Mild…" Transformation involved meeting the other and being mightily disturbed.

A Theological Anthropology for Formation for Christian Spirituality

The "other" is a call, a liturgy, a sacrament, a promise of God's work of transformation in our lives that reveals the meaning of our existence. This, I believe are basic tenets of Christian anthropology and therefore also the basis for formation for Christian spirituality. Ultimately, we can only know who we are in the light of encountering the "other" in the man Jesus the Messiah. This was Karl Barth's fundamental point about theological anthropology.[8] We cannot figure out who we are and what we are about by our own means, we need to encounter Jesus the Messiah through hearing the story of the Gospels. The great achievements of science can tell us about a process of physical development, the great evolution of creation, what it cannot tell us is who we are and what our destiny is and what we are to become. This insight can only come to us in encounter with the "other" in Jesus the Messiah who is intrinsically linked to the "other" in our neighbour and creation. In him we see who we are destined to be – who we are to become. The feeble attempts human self-reliance – the idea that humankind has come of age – due to the era of the enlightenment signalled by the philosopher Emmanuel Kant (1724-1804), or Nietzche's (1844-1900) atheistic humanism in the "übermensch" (the "over-man" or "super-man") and the way this led to its final expression in the mass killing of twentieth century wars and genocides only underline this truth.[9] Karl Barth wanted to oppose what he called "absolute man" that he saw arise out of these movements. For Barth the Christian Gospel had to counter this idea" of the human person in its "bodily passions" of self-reliance and self-absorption that was so confidently announced by Immanuel Kant and others. For Barth the only counter to this human folly is to emphasise that the revelation of who we are and what we are about comes from God. It is in the redemptive office of Jesus the Messiah that we discover our own office – our own place in life.[10] We cannot find our true identity and destiny in the "wisdom of this age."

This claim, which holds much theological water, returns us to the tension between human agency and God's action. Barth wanted theological anthropology to be rooted first in the content of the work of Jesus as the Messiah and the revelatory power of the Gospel story. We have to listen and hear the call and understand the logic of God's covenant to know ourselves. This is a profound and valid concern. That is why I have structured this book to start with "Call" and "Listen".

Paul Tillich felt that this idea, that we discover truth in our encounter with God, limits God too much. Between Tillich and Barth I argue for the importance of the mediation of encounter with the Messiah (with Barth) but with

Tillich I want to qualify this encounter as mediated through our fellow humans and perhaps even through our encounter with creation. What Barth has not attended to is how Jesus is reported to describe an encounter of God as deeply and integrally connected to an encounter of love and service with our suffering neighbour? Of course our encounter with God never makes us know all of God but it allows us to know enough. Tillich's concept of "absolute faith" which he argues transcends the divine-human encounter is meant to emphasise that God is beyond the personal.[11] Of course, we can agree that God's being far transcends our encounter and experience of God, yet, there appears to be something fundamental of God that is revealed through encounter. This personal encounter, relationship, and community between God and people is one of the great themes of the Hebrew and Christian Scriptures! I do not believe that acknowledging that God is more than encounter means that our human condition in meeting God in encounter should be seen as inadequate. In fact, in the very encounter, we know that we encounter more than we expected. Walking in covenant relationship and living in the habit of covenant faithfulness is the way we grasp God. In this, God, as we saw in chapters one and two, is always the subject, the prime actor, the first one to move in grace towards us.

However, we have to ask if it is as simple as Barth seems to imply? Can revelation "from above" or "from beyond" really be separated from the complexity of our experience of life? Does it really drop into our consciousness like a meteorite from the God dimension without any reference point? Is the image of God in which we are created as community so utterly destroyed that no sliver of light falls in from our creaturely existence? How do we acknowledge the otherness and "beyondness" of God in relation to the limitation of human experience and language? We have to ask these questions if we are to think responsibly of formation for Christian spirituality.

What is this human being we encounter on our way on earth? What is this being that we are? Our reflection in Chapter 1 pointed us to the hints in the Genesis 1 narrative that the image of God is captured exactly in our creation as creatures in community there expressed metaphorically in the community of man and woman. The point here is not the elevation of biological sexual difference as essential to community, but rather that God's image is carried in a community that transcends the isolated human person by celebrating being together in difference. It is this community that is damaged in the act of human rebellion and that leads to our fundamental alienation.[12] It appears that our redemption lies in a knowing and encountering the other in God's great covenant plan. This is what makes Jesus' story of the Great Judgement in Matthew 25:31ff. such a seminal story. In this story Jesus refuses to divorce love and care for the neighbour, particularly the neighbour that is most vulnerable and reviled, from the ultimate redemptive embrace of God. There is no mere spiritual salvation here, the soul is not just saved through a formulaic prayer, but we are judged in the light of our journey to the neighbour and our doing of justice. Encounter with the Messiah – the Son of Man – is mediated through our loving and serving encounter with the marginalised in society. To know God, to know Jesus, is to know and love our neighbour in their most vulnerable state. We find who we are through encounter in love with our neighbour and thus we encounter the Messiah – God. It is in this final judgement – the eschatological moment when we stand before the "Son of Man"– that we know to what extent we have truly known and followed the Messiah.

Barth is right, we discover who we are only as we encounter Jesus the Messiah in his redemptive office. However, I have to add, that we encounter him through the journey towards loving and caring for our most vulnerable neighbour and creation! N.T. Wright, in his recent reflection on Paul's theology of justification by faith, argues that in the Pauline account there are consistently two moves related to God's redemptive work in us. First we find God's initial justifying judgement in Jesus the Messiah that declares us justified despite our covenant unfaithfulness. We are declared justified in God's Divine court because Jesus the man is faithful to the covenant. Second, we are on a journey towards the final eschaton in which the final judgement will occur, there God's judgement will be a judgement of "works" that will gauge if we have walked in his Spirit. This judgement, as Paul imagine it, is a purifying and transformative judgement rather than a rejecting judgement (see 2 Cor. 3:18). Thus, even though we are declared justified, we are to work out our salvation in fear and trembling for it is God who is at work in us through the Spirit of the Messiah (Phil 2:12-13). This working out occurs in the journey of loving service to the vulnerable in whom, time and again, we encounter the Messiah in and through whom we know who we truly are. This is the habit of working hard on the way...

Without repeating Wright's persuasive argument completely, we do need to note that he emphasises that we are dealing here not with "works" as merit but with "works" as in the logic of love. The work and love of the Spirit inspire us to encounter our most vulnerable neighbour and to care for them and to draw them into community with God and ourselves. In this way we are enabled to become covenant-faithful.[13] In addition we need to note that the eschatological Judge (in Matthew the Son of Man), is associated in the Gospels and in Paul and in apocalyptic texts in the Hebrew Scriptures with the Messiah. The one who judges is also the one who empowers by his Spirit and the one that died on our behalf and rose again. The final Judge is indeed grace embodied. Our journey to the neighbour as a journey to Jesus the Messiah and God, is a journey that falls under the rubric of the love of God and neighbour, and it is in this journey and encounter, enlightened by the Gospel narratives, that we find ourselves. This is the heart of a theological anthropology of formation for Christian spirituality. If we understand the meaning of our being as something discovered on this journey, it suggests that for us to live in Christian spirituality is to hear the call and invitation which invites us to engage this journey towards God and our neighbours.

In some ways the observations above are a long way from the theology of Paul Tillich. We should observe first that Tillich works with a very different understanding of how God is revealed to us from that of Barth. He attempts to take the route into the depth human experience and the Western philosophical traditions to understand how God is mediated to us through the plumbing of the depths of human existence. This presents us with the flip side of the claim of a revelation from beyond (or "above"). Although Tillich himself did not completely reject the emphasis of his contemporary European theologians on the importance of the encounter with God, as we have seen above, he does deem this encounter to be less decisive and preliminary to the more profound process of what he calls 'absolute faith'.[14] He argued that understanding and being ourselves (the courage to be), ultimately derives from being grasped by the God beyond theism, the One who appears when the God of theism has disappeared in anxiety of doubt.[15] Tillich's solution of "absolute faith", deeply rooted in the Lutheran understanding of the confidence of faith in the face of all objections, and in response to 20th century existential philosophy, does carry a strong intellectual middle class and perhaps predominantly male grasp of the challenges, issues of life, and angst. The marginalised and godless hungry and persecuted peoples of the world are not necessarily grappling with meaninglessness, but rather with survival and hopelessness of another order. Nevertheless, we have to remember that Tillich's concern remained focused on the problem of both the otherness and the "with-in-and-with-us-ness" of God. His valid concern was that we would make our human symbols into God. This he rightly pointed out is idolatry. Such idolatry is most common when fundamentalist forms of faith make their system into a kind of pseudo-god.

What is important here for our understanding of Christian spirituality on the journey is Tillich's analysis of the two dimensions of human existence; **participating as part of the whole** (or collective) and **asserting self as separate**. His description of both these movements in the human condition is convincing and helpful in building a vision of human anthropology and journey. Tillich's assertion that faith is not simply about encounter but about process or dynamic movement is also extremely important.[16] We discover who we really are in engaging the world and others. In fact, we find our identity as human beings in relationship. Through the other we discover the ground of our being who is Christ and through Christ we discover God. These insights seem to me to be very much a reflection of the Gospel assertion (Matthew 25) that we are known by the eschatological Judge (The Messiah and ultimately God) as we move towards the need of our neighbour, particularly our vulnerable and suffering neighbour. Tillich is right that such a movement to the other and others, is one of self-abandonment (think of the habit of self-giving sacrifice), and his is also right that we cannot do so without also knowing ourselves as self in relation to other.[17] This, as Emmanuel Levinas, the Lithuanian philosopher claims, is indeed a **meontology** (something that is before being – we need this before we can be), a me-ontology of the human person. I claim here that discovering who we are – finding our ontology, destiny, and meaning – is not a boundless self-assertion in the face of anxiety and doubt in Tillich's mode of "absolute faith", but rather a function of the courage to be for the other – to *kneel before the other* as Levinas' puts it.[18] This is a grounded process of the journey towards the other while also discovering ourselves as self. This is the habit of covenant faithfulness.

Contemporary philosophers such as Judith Butler has pointed out how much of who we are is constructed under the constraint of the cultural world we live in. It is therefore important not to be tempted by either Barth or Tillich to think that we become and learn to see and understand ourselves in a vacuum. Engagement with the world and others can also warp us away from relationship and love. It is particularly in the encounter and journey with those people, animals and plants that are most vulnerable that we can grow and become full and meaningful creatures as humans.

Tillich is right in observing that within such a process of participation and self-affirmation we are always encountering something beyond the process. He is also right in being concerned that our encounters with others and God as the "Other" may be wrongly taken by us as an absolute that becomes an idol thus losing the otherness and beyondness of God. Tillich suspects that if we make our encounters too absolute we diminish God and we ultimately lose a dimension of who we are ourselves. But, as he observes himself, all religious experience, all true "*ecstasis*" (dynamic beyondness) contain the awareness of the "*musterion tremendum et facinosum*" (the fearful and fascinating mystery); it contains both the annihilating power and elevating power of God.[19] God encountered in call, God listened to in narrative, God in the poor, suffering and the vulnerable, God observed and sacramentally tasted, seen, smelled and heard in the Messiah, leads us on a journey through others and through God to ourselves.

These digressions and critiques of the insights of Barth and Tillich help us construct a theology of the person that sheds light on our task of formation for Christian spirituality. It is in Jesus the Messiah, the encounter with him through the vulnerable, and the history of the narratives that tell his story, that we find ourselves. Finding ourselves is a journey. It is a journey to the other, particularly the other as the one in need, the other before whom we kneel in loving self-donation, the other who mediates our dynamic and ongoing encounter with Jesus the Messiah. With Tillich we affirm that this journey is the journey of participation. This journey of participation also confronts us with ourselves as being as self. The process of participation and self-affirmation is an inseparable one, and also a continuous circular one that engages others as well as disengages to affirm self. In the engagement with the other we see Jesus the Messiah more clearly, and know God in encounter. This encounter is both annihilating (overwhelming, awesome, and always mysterious) and elevating.

We are called on this journey of engagement and discovery wherein our meaning lies. I assert here that the despair, anxiety and doubt that Tillich so eloquently expose in human experience is met not by the type of "absolute faith" that he suggests, but rather with faith expressed in engagement on the journey. It is stepping out on the journey to the other that is the expression of the courage to be in the Christian sense of the word. It is thus the ongoing journey of repentance. Formation for Christian spirituality is nothing less than inviting and accompanying others on this journey of repentance. It is therefore not an irrational leap of faith, it is a walking towards the other who is in need.

It is important here to note Tillich's brilliant analysis of the nature of North American society and its own way of dealing with anxiety about faith and meaninglessness. He observes that this North American way is to deal with anxiety by believing in engagement with the productive process of competitive society. Perhaps we can add to this that today it is further expressed in consumerism and it is no less pervasive today, than in Tillich's time. This kind of "*productive optimism*" and "*shopping as life*" idea must in no way be confused with the courage to engage the journey towards the other and oneself. North American churches tend to be deeply compromised by productive optimism and consumer attitudes. Tillich argues that, in the North American context, a destructive fusion occurs between two very different dimensions of life. During the Renaissance – the era between the 14th and 17th centuries in Europe in which people harked back to ancient literature and art as ideal – people saw themselves as part of a creative process that engages creation and its forces. However, the North American culture involves the mixing of this Renaissance synthesis with being an autonomous being in the North American competitive-productive process.[20] In North American culture this strange mixture is made possible by the transformation and denial of death achieved by making death into a mask of the productive society itself. This process is supported by a kind of belief in the immortality of the soul that is neither Christian nor Neo-Platonic.[21] The great Renaissance depiction of the human at the helm of a sailing ship with fate blowing in the sails was for the Renaissance person a creative engagement with life, but for the North American person holding the helm is engaging and controlling production. We can thus conclude that we have moved from a sensitive balance between human agency and the powers of creation around us, in the Renaissance vision of life, to an exploitative power exercised by human manipulation and mastery over creation. The destructive effect of this shift is all too obvious today in our vulnerable and crumbling biosphere. The habits of covenant faithfulness and self-giving sacrifice run counter to this.

It is therefore important to emphasise that the courage to journey towards the other as our neighbour is not about productivity and the boundless optimism of heaping production on production, but about engaging the other with love and creativity. So much of what is called church in North America is a parody of the productive person of North American democracy. In this distorted form it is about finding productive forms of organising and entertaining, and perhaps even manipulating people in a community that is erroneously named "church". Elsewhere I have argued that this production focused obsession can be captured in the idea of mastery. The confusion of efficiency and production – human mastery – with fellow human engagement is one of the core idols of North American society. Forming people for Christian spirituality is accompanying and leading others away from such idolatry. It is a constant process of repentance.

The Crucified Messiah and our Identity

In his book *The Courage to Be* Tillich writes about the kind of church that rightly expresses its role and place in the world,

> It is the Church under the Cross which alone can do this, the Church which preaches the Crucified who cried to God who remained his God after the God of confidence had left him in the darkness of doubt and meaninglessness.[22]

Although Tillich does not unpack this statement in great detail, his sentiment is clear. He is trying to emphasise that it is in the vulnerability of Jesus the Messiah and in its expression on the cross that we find the Gospel that the Church has to preach. Formation for Christian spirituality on the journey is of necessity and expression of the work of the church and an expression of this same Gospel. We cannot claim that we find our human identity and meaning in Jesus the Messiah without noting both the importance of the cross (mortification) and the resurrection (vivification) for our understanding of the human person and that person's formation for Christian spirituality. Of course, the agony of the cross, and the meaning of the cry of Jesus, "My God my God why have you forsaken me" (Mark 15:4), is open to interpretation and Tillich reads it in the context of his own argument marked by existential philosophy. His interpretation certainly contains a significant part of the meaning of this moment in the story of the Gospel yet there is more. What does this moment of mortification and the experience of God-forsakenness of Jesus mean for our own theology of the human being? How does this event enlighten us about our own meaning and meaninglessness?

The Journey Through God-Forsakenness

The Reformed Theologian Jürgen Moltmann (1926-) argues that the cross event is the beginning of the history of God. The experience of the forsakenness of Jesus the Messiah on this cross ("My God, my God, why have you forsaken me?) is in fact the revelatory core of who God is as Trinitarian God. In this moment all dimensions of God is revealed. Jesus the Messiah (the Son) is bereft of God, the Father is torn away from the Son, and the Spirit grieves in the tearing open of God with the Father and the Son. This moment reveals God, it also reveals who we are in relation to the dying and rising Messiah. God is a community and communion of Father, Son and Spirit. In correspondence to this community of God we echo God in human community. I argued in chapter one how male and female as community becomes a metaphor for the image of God in human community. This communal character of God and humans carries another dimension of a theology of the human person.

First, however, we need to begin with the cruciform nature of the revelation of God in the cross event. The anxiety of the human condition, or its challenge to live and hope in the face of forsakenness, is taken up into God-self on the cross. God enters this God-forsaken state. In Jesus on the cross God-self enters Godlessness. That is why the Father and the Son **have** to be torn apart. The rebellion and waywardness of the human condition and its self-assertion in complete self-reliance – hubris – is negated and absorbed into God-self on the cross. When the facts demand death, God insists on life for God's creatures! God-self is mortified on the cross to share all our destitution as rebellious creatures. Jesus the Messiah loses meaning and relationship with the Father yet persists faithfully (covenant faithfulness) in the face of it. This leads to the verdict – "you are truly righteous" – of resurrection. It is in this Gospel mortification and vivification that we see our meaning as human beings, and it is in engaging the journey towards the other expressed in God's journey towards us in the Messiah that we find our vocation. This means that our human condition is marked by a cruciform reality and our vocation and meaning is embraced in following the cruciform journey towards the other and ultimately towards God. We give ourselves (loving self-giving sacrifice) in mortification and we are made alive (vivified) in God's gracious judgement over us "you are truly righteous because of Jesus the Messiah."

The resurrection is as important as death in the story of our being. Central to the story of Jesus is the clear meaning assigned to his bodily resurrection. The implications are the establishment of a new order, and the constitution of a calling and a sending of humankind under God's coming reign. N.T. Wright describes the key place of the resurrection in this story as "watershed stuff".[23] He writes,

> This is a million miles from the hymns that speak of Jesus' resurrection in terms of our own assurance of a safe and happy rest in heaven. Quite the contrary. Jesus' resurrection summons us to dangerous and difficult tasks on earth.[24]

And, we should add, it summons us to a journey to our neighbour, the nations and, as we will see now, the cosmos. Responding to the summons and engagement with this journey tells us who we are.

The Journey to the Cosmos

> For God so loved the cosmos that God gave God's only Son... (John 3:16 author's translation)
> This plan, which God will complete when the time is right, is to bring all creation together, everything in heaven and on earth, with Christ as head. (Eph 1:10 GNB)

So far we have explored the theology of the human person in relation to other people. Earlier we argued that God's act of creation is the original act of mission. As we think of our identity in Christian spirituality it is now important to realise that the broken human community, *and* the broken whole of creation is now the object of God's redemptive mission that we are called to join. We are called and sent. We are sent, not only to the other in person, but also to the whole cosmos. Nothing less than the renewal of all things, the bringing together (*anakephalaiomai*) of all that exists in creation is what our sending is about (Eph. 1:10). A theology of the human person that remains only human focused will miss the essential place and role, and thus the meaning, of who we are created to be. We are created for community *and* we are created to serve and to protect creation[25].

Being sent to do this is not only our work, this is first of all God's work, but if we continue to read Ephesians 1, from which we cite above, we discover in verse 18 that we have a hope of our calling – a calling to the love of neighbour and the tending of creation. We are called to the nations (*panta ta ethne* Mat 28:19), to the whole world (*eis ton kosmon apanta* Mark 16:15), and in a process of being *witnesses* on a journey to new places (Jerusalem, all of Judea, Samaria and to the utter and absolute end – *eschatou tes ges* Acts 1:8). We are therefore on an eschatological journey to the nations and to the cosmos. We are called into being and sent to marginalised people, the nations, and the cosmos to love and to serve in cruciform ways for the bringing together of all things in God. Formation for Christian spirituality is formation on this journey of mission.

> "Do not eat that part of the fish", counselled the pastor earnestly, "it is dangerous, it is polluted by the nuclear tests at Mururoa…" I was on Rangiroa, an atoll island in the South Pacific, and cast upon the hospitality of the pastor to a small community of believers who eked out a living in this remote part of the world. Surely this was something like going to the utter end (*eschatou* Acts 1:8) of the world? In front of me was my breakfast and the whole family was watching me earnestly. It was a raw fish, freshly caught and placed neatly in the middle of my plate with the dead eye coldly staring at me. Shortly after I arrived I realised that they had purchased very expensive canned food to feed me as part of their hospitality. I immediately assured them that I will eat what they eat, I will live with them as they do… Now I had to put the raw fish where my mouth was! Besides losing some weight on this sojourn in the South Pacific, I gained more than I could ever imagine. Every part of my consumer self-absorbed Western culture, narrow theology, and life-style was being challenged. "Do you realise that the French have polluted and destroyed our food and endangered our children with their

nuclear tests?" I was asked. "Why do you only cook only for yourselves?" I was asked another curious Polynesian, "Surely you need more in case a guest arrives?" "Why do people in the West commit suicide?" a mother asked. "Don't they have families to love them?" "Why do you want us to be quiet when you have a head-ache?" a youth asked me with great puzzlement, "Surely, the group is more important than the individual?" "Why do you European Christians judge gay people" asked an older pastor, "we have always recognised that some people are different and that they have a place in our community..." In my youthful enthusiasm I trained a group of teens to act out some of the Gospel stories. When they enacted the great judgement and the sheep were separated from the goats, the twelve year old who played the eschatological judge, burst into tears. "How could God do this? I cannot reject my friends", he sobbed. Then he herded all the "goats" to the gracious and loving embrace of the Judge. Now, some thirty years later, these pivotal questions still remain with me and shape me wherever I go. I was transformed only in a small way, yet somehow something did change...

Geographic and cultural journeys are a key part of the spiritual journey and ultimately the journey to knowing who we are and what we are about. Such journeys bring us to participation in the world and communities we encounter and they bring us to becoming ourselves. In Tillich's terms they make possible both "participation in" and "being as self". What the missional and inter-cultural nature of such journeys add to Tillich's Eurocentric and Androcentric vision is the challenge of the other as completely different and the challenge of the cosmos as suffering, sighing and groaning. Such journeys are therefore in my view critical to understanding who we are as humans and who Christ is and these journeys are essential to formation for Christian spirituality.

For those of us in multi-cultural contexts such journeys may not require a long geographic leg; it might simply be a journey to the house next door, yet without them we will not be formed well for our vocation and we will be impoverished in our Christian spirituality. Without them fundamental questions and critical insights might pass us by and we might know less of who we are. Without our own *perigrinatio pro Christi* we may never be able to journey back to neighbours like ourselves and see them with new eyes of love and faith. Without such *perigrinatio* to the biosphere polluted by the arrogance of our nuclear tests, and green house gasses, we will never know that the poor are the first to suffer under the burden of our self-assured and self-reliant technological obsession. If we do not journey to Africa we might never know that this continent that has a small contribution to pollution is the worst effected by the pollution of the rest of the world with deserts growing and forests and arable land disappearing. Like Columba's Iona of old, formation for Christian spirituality thus needs to stand in the sign of the White Monastery (self-giving sacrificial journey for the Gospel)[26] – preparing and exposing us to self-giving and self-challenging journeys.

It takes more than a journey to change us. We may engage a journey while remaining closed to its lessons. We may travel to other places simply to confirm our own prejudices and many do. We may go to tell others that we know better than them. Formation for Christian spirituality challenges us to seek the habit of openness, the habit of the Gospel-heart that journeys with the expectation to be challenged and changed rather than with the expectation to have our own perspective confirmed. The Gospel-heart witnesses in humility rather than in triumphalism. It is journey in the habit of having our mind transformed in self-giving worship. As with our conclusion on the importance of journeying in love to be open and to serve our neighbour and those who are most vulnerable, so it is with the geographic journey.

We do travel as witnesses, but we travel as witnesses who know our task. Our witness is to the one who gave himself – to the self-emptying God. Our witness is in the cruciform nature of those on a journey for the bringing together of all things. Our witness is embodied in taking on communion with those to whom we journey, even as God chose to take on communion with being human a culture, a people and a biosphere. Our witness is incarnational albeit only a shadow of the true incarnation. David Bosch reflects on the paradox of our witness and the tension between certainty and openness in this way,

> "Such language boils down to an admission that we do not have all the answers ... This is not opting for agnosticism, but for humility. It is, however, bold humility – or a humble boldness. We know only in part, but we do know. And we believe that the faith we profess is both true and just, and should be proclaimed. We do this, however, not as judges or lawyers, but as witnesses; not as soldiers, but as envoys of peace; not as high-pressure salespersons, but as ambassadors of the Servant of the Lord."[27]

Journey, Human Development and Formation

Lest we forget that life journeys are also journeys of development and change in people we need to attend to the importance of human development for our grasp of formation on a journey. At 18 years old I was at a stage in my life in my own culture where the task before me was to find my own being as self in a formative and critical way. When I was invited to the black township in South Africa, this journey to be "as self" coincided with a process of participation in the world of another culture and in the presence of oppression. This journey created an indelible imprint in my process of personal growth. The formative journey of encounter – participation in – coincided with the formative journey of being "as self".

Educational theorists have long studied the developmental journey of people from being an infant to adulthood and beyond. Even though stage theories of development all hold their own assumptions and commitments to particular psychological schools, they do speak of a universal experience of growth and development in the human person. These theories also observe the human possibilities and limitations at different ages and stages of life. Systems such as Object Relations Theory have established a theoretical framework for the development of the human person to mature adulthood (object constancy in its jargon) and tools for analysis of fractures in this process of development where critical formative parental relationships become toxic.

Other authors, such as Daniel Levinson, studied the male journey of development in North American society identifying tasks and struggles in different stages of life right to old age.[28] Carol Gilligan, through meticulous research, has shown that moral development in girls and women seems to differ from that in boys and men.[29] Of course, such theories must be read and understood in cultural context and are profoundly impacted by the constructions and sometimes the biases of cultures and their power brokers. There are very different processes of human development in different cultures. Differentiation form the parent, so highly valued in Anglo-Saxon culture and often made into a doctrine in North American psychology, is not necessarily appropriate in the same way in Mediterranean, African or Eastern cultures. The culture specific elements of human development theory and the culture and context specific quality of cultural constructions of human experience thus make it hard to generalise on human development as an overarching theory beyond the biology of physical traits and brain function. However, that people need to grow and find themselves within their own cultural context over time from infanthood to adulthood and through stages of ageing is true for all cultures. The recognition and attention to this human condition of development is essential for formation for Christian spirituality.

What we can say with some certainty is that any process of formation for Christian spirituality needs to work at being culturally appropriate. At the same time it should also unceasingly ask if a particular cultural construction serve loving freedom in communion? The task of recognising and respecting difference while bringing people together under God's call and covenant, is not an optional extra, it goes to the very Gospel message itself. It is about God's-promise-through-Abraham's-family-for-the-world (see Chapter 2). It is exactly in showing respect and care for cultural difference that we express the bringing of God's blessings to all nations. Each culture will have its own ways of participation and being "as self", and will have its own understanding of how this process works through the life-cycle of people. Each culture, including one's own, always contain its own idolatries and brilliant insights and the conversation among cultures is one essential way to discover both the glory and the darkness of one's own cultural assumptions. As we lead and accompany people from different cultures on the journey of formation for Christian spirituality, listening carefully and sharing the dimensions of different cultural perceptions are an essential part of the process and an expression of the Gospel. Such a process of inter-cultural exploration of growth and development challenges participants from all cultures to turn away from the hubris of absolutising a particular culture. In the history of the expansion of the Christian faith one of its most spectacular successes has been its ability to contextualise in different cultures. At the same time this is also the area in which the church failed miserably, particularly in the colonial missionary era when European culture was made normative. The critiques of post-colonial authors (people who critique the way Western culture and values were forced on other cultures of the world)[30] is therefore of great help as we think of formation for Christian spirituality.

The Theology of the Human Person-community and Formation

The exploration of the chapter so far is a discovery of the meaning of the human person as person formed on a journey. In it I have argued for a conception of the human person in terms of the metaphor of journey. This is a journey of relationship in time and space and physical journey in body, culture, and cosmos. In all these dimensions the spiritual journey cannot be divorced from our embodied existence in creation. We have found a long Christian tradition of journey represented beautifully in the story of God's journey to humankind in the incarnation. We have also noted the journeys of faith of important biblical figures and the journeys of early Christians, the journeys of monasticism and mission through the ages. In the light of this we have argued for the revealing power of engaging the other, the nations and the cosmos on our journey.

We suggested, following Barth, that we know who we are only in the light of Jesus the Messiah and his office as a human person. We have also argued that we encounter Jesus the Messiah in the journey to the other, particularly the other as marginalised. In addition, we find our meaning and purpose as human beings in the journey to the nations and the cosmos for the eschatological bringing together of all things. The nature of this journey includes the journey of participation in the world and the journey of being as ourselves. These two parts of the journey, as we have learned from Paul Tillich, are inseparable. However, the courage to be, which expresses faith and hope, is found in engaging the journey in the face of, in spite of, in contradiction of, all cynicism, hopelessness and meaninglessness and ultimately suffering that may confront us. This means that we engage the journey in a cruciform way as we follow the Messiah. This, we can add here is the meaning of the Christian symbol of martyrdom or, as Paul puts it in Romans 8:17 "sharing Christ's suffering". Our call and our mission, to be sent are inextricably linked to who we are as human beings. Formation for Christian spirituality requires this fundamental journeying character of the human condition and invites, accompanies, and leads others on this journey as the act of formation.

At this point it is becoming clear that the term formation is a deficient one. The word formation implies that there is a kind of technology of one forming another. Formation is not first of all an institutional or even a human task executed on another. Whether teachers or whether communities of faith, we cannot form another person, neither can we impact them sufficiently to call it formation. We do not call and we do not transform. We cannot engineer formation and there is no technology of formation that can be captured. Formation is ultimately a journey in which God is more than subject and object in relation to the human person. When and if we conceive formation as something done with and to a person then we need to insist that it is ultimately God who forms. In the words of the prophet, God is the potter; we are the clay (Is. 64:8). It is God who calls and sends, it is God who encounters the one called, and it is God by the Spirit who transforms, reshapes, forgives, justifies, and loves us into being on the journey. This insight is reflected in the call of Abraham explored in Chapter Two. This story emphasises this initiative from God in contrast to the human attempt to attain "instant formation" in knowing good and evil in the story of the Garden of Eden. It is God who will make us, magnify our names, God will bless those who bless us, and God will deal with those who don't.

The task of accompanying and perhaps leading others on the journey of Christian spirituality is a very humble one. This task is one of being a witness, a fellow traveller, and of a fellow discerner – being a companion on the way. We do not call, but we can witness to call and discern with great trepidation together as a community if a call and a gift is present. Most of all we can travel with the one called as fellow traveller and bring the witness of our own engagement, friendship and discernment to that journey. It is in our own faithfulness to call that we can witness to and accompany others on their journey. It is in our own engagement with the "other" and community and cosmos that we can discern the call together in prayer and fasting.

We have to ask if this emphasis on the humble place of our task in relation to the initiative that comes from God does not contradict our conclusions on the importance of human agency and fostering spiritual habits in the previous chapter? The response has to be of the same nature as in the last chapter. The duality between God's action and ours is something that does not seem to occur in Paul's conception of the work of the Christian community. Working out our salvation with fear in trembling is in fact a reflection of God at will and work within us. Thus we see the humble place of our task in formation, yet we engage it with utmost vigour, care and love.

The Journey Towards the Coming Reign of God

> This, then, is how you should pray: 'Our Father in heaven: May your holy name be honoured; may your Kingdom come; may your will be done on earth as it is in heaven.
> Jesus (Mat. 6:9, GNB)

So far we have emphasised the embodied and sacramental nature of the journey of Christian formation. Matter matters. The physical creation has been created good and so space, time, and matter are all part of the renewing purpose of God. The kingdom that is at hand and is to come, comes in the context of all that exists, both heaven and earth. Jesus' arch-prayer teaches this dramatically. Note how the prayer for the coming kingdom is followed by the prayer for bread which feeds our embodied nature. As we have seen earlier, our journey is an eschatological one calling us towards the end that God purposes, and this journey brings us face to face with our existence as part of the matter of creation, subject to the space in which we live and move and determined by time. As with the habits of Christian disposition, so it is in our journey towards and for the coming reign of God – human agency and Divine initiative are to be understood in their proper relationship. We do not inaugurate the reign of God. We do not make it happen or start it. We do not make it come through our world changing initiatives. It has begun in the coming of Jesus the Messiah. Jesus is clear in his invitation to the disciples after announcing that the kingdom is already at hand, they are to follow him in it. Our effort to follow, transformative and world changing as it should be, is thus in response to the reign of God which has come and is coming. The fruit of our actions, if met with God's approval, are provisional signs of the coming reign. There is effort on our side, there is a journey to make. As N.T. Wright puts it,

> But what we can and must do in the present, if we are obedient to the gospel, if we are following Jesus, and if we are indwelt, energized, and directed by the Spirit, is to build *for* the kingdom.[31]

In the Gospel of Matthew, the Sermon on the Mount is placed following the invitation to the disciples to follow. It provides rubrics for the signs of the reign of God. In the domain of God's reign these are the signs: valuing, the poor, the meek, those who mourn, purity, the quest for justice and holiness, and the persecuted and oppressed. Building for the reign of God involves journeying with the same values and working for the objectives of purity, justice, and holiness while bearing the marks of costly witness. In our journey towards the other, the poor, the marginalised, the suffering, and the sighing creation we act in the spirit of the Sermon on the Mount. Wright has unpacked these signs of the reign of God in which we build in terms of the concepts of justice, beauty and evangelism. Each concept provides us with a dimension of the journey. It tells us what the eschatological journey that builds for the reign of God aims for. To be formed for Christian spirituality on the journey is to walk this way symbolised by the words of Jesus, "Come, follow me…"

The Constructive Journey for God's Reign of Justice

The Greek word *dikaiosyne* and all its forms in the New Testament is a very hard one to translate. Earlier, I painted the use of this word in the Sermon of the Mount with the English word justice. We briefly discussed the broadness of this idea in Chapter two. The common translation with the English word righteousness has been spiritualised in Christian circles to the point that it often loses its concrete dimensions such as liberation of the poor, hungry and oppressed and the care and protection of the the widow and the orphan. Too many times in South Africa I was confronted with a pious "white" concept of righteousness that was not one wit concerned with the oppression of millions of black people.

> Rosina Mpashlele disappeared. Rosina was the representative elder in my Presbytery (a regional governing body in the Presbyterian church consisting of local elders and ministers). The week before there was a youth protest march in Rosina's township. When the po-

lice turned up with guns and live ammunition Rosina saw the danger of violence and killing. A grandmother of some 63 years of age
at the time, she marched in between the frontlines of the unarmed
youth and the police with their guns, masks, batons and shields. She
carried nothing in her hands, but put her body between the con-
fronting groups inviting the police, made up of white men, to listen
and to talk to the black youth on the other side. She was grabbed by
a police officer and after that no one could tell what happened to her.
We enquired in different places. The police would neither confirm
nor deny that they had taken her. They held all the power with the
right to imprison indefinitely without charge and without explanation. This meant that people simply "disappeared". After all known
avenues of inquiry were exhausted the moderator of my Presbytery
asked if I would speak to an important and influential man in the
white Dutch Reformed Church to ask if he would intervene on our
behalf with the government to trace our friend and fellow Christian.
We met and after telling him about the disappearance he told me that
he would do nothing because, "if the police took her she must have
done something wrong." After several weeks of searching we finally
traced her to a local prison and representatives of the Presbytery were
allowed to visit Rosina. She was in solitary confinement, her glasses
were broken and without it she could not read. Her action was considered "political" and "un-spiritual". Such an experience casts new
light for me on Jesus' words "blessed are the peacemakers..."

David Bosch, no stranger to the warped expressions of "righteousness" in the
South African context, examined the concepts of the kingdom of God (*basileia*)
and justice-righteousness (*dikaiosyne*) particularly as they appear in the Gospel
of Matthew[32]. Matthew is arguably the Gospel of the Kingdom because it contains the most references to God's kingdom mainly titled the "kingdom of heav-
en" with "heaven" most likely serving as a euphemism for God. Bosch points
out that Matthew refers to preaching the "Gospel of the Kingdom" which
for him means encountering Jesus the Messiah.[33] Matthew seems to have a
unique way of using the concept *dikaiosyne* that contrasts with his sources.
The three possible translations of *dikaiosyne* are justification, righteousness or
justice. The choice made in translation can have radical results. Simply reading through Matthew and replacing the traditional translation "righteousness"
with "justice" is quite a revealing exercise! However, Bosch, following Michael
Crosby argues that we should not choose among these possible translations,

but rather, that we should recognise the multiple dimensions to its meaning in the Matthean text. In this Crosby and Bosch go back to Isaiah 61 to read both a constitutive and normative dimension into the meaning of the word *dikaiosyne*[34].

Returning to Isaiah for unpacking *dikaiosyne* makes sense because of the large shadow this text casts over both Matthew 5 and Luke 4. It makes it impossible to simply spiritualise the poor, the meek, and the mourning. The strong embrace of the broken hearted, the proclamation of good news to the poor and liberty to the captives and unjustly imprisoned are clearly signs of the reign of God inaugurated by the coming of the Messiah. It supports neither a blind justice of the judicial kind, nor a spiritualised righteousness disembodied from action. In fact, *dikaiosyne* read in this light speaks of the action of love. It is the kind of action that can get one into trouble if you ask questions and challenge the injustice that keeps oppression going. It is empathic spiritual justice marked by holiness; it is being different from the world around us. It is a justice that lives out of the world to come not out of the spirit of the present age. It is justice practiced in love, hope and faith. Bosch describes this reading of *dikaiosyne* as "faith in action, the practice of devotion."[35] Bosch writes,

> Matthew's pleas for a justice that "surpasses" that of the Pharisees and for being "perfect" have to be seen in the same light. It makes no sense to see these injunctions in the context of moral superiority or higher accomplishments. …. The rich young man was not just asked to give all his possessions to the poor, but also to follow Jesus. The latter summons is the really decisive one; the "being perfect" manifests itself in discipleship.[36]

The journey of following, building, and acting for the reign of God is thus engaged under this kind of righteousness. It follows the habits of eschatological living and self-giving sacrifice.

The Constructive Journey for God's Reign of Beauty

I concur with N.T. Wright that a revitalised focus on the aesthetic is necessary for our understanding of journeying and working for the reign of God. There are of course no neat Bible passages to point us directly in this way. Jesus did not include, "Blessed are those who create beauty" in the beatitudes! Yet, there are many reasons why Beauty cannot be neglected as part of our journey in following Jesus the Messiah in building for the reign of God.

We must, with N.T. Wright, start with a theology off creation.[37] The cherishment of the good creation in the original creation account and the beauty of the renewed creation depicted in the book of revelation, or the wonder of the resurrected body contemplated by Paul all point us towards the creation of beauty as a kingdom reflecting activity. In fact the Hebrew word which is translated in the refrain, "And God saw that it was good" in Genesis 1 is a word that communicates aesthetic beauty and rightness rather than moral rectitude.

We find of course much beauty in the Scriptures themselves, including the prayers and hymns of the Psalms, the beauty of prose, and the fascinating depth of the language like that of the Gospel of John. Psalms and spiritual songs are mentioned by Paul as important worship activities point to the beauty of poetry and music that can express some of the depths of creative potential under God's reign.

Christian tradition, despite its concern about idolatry, where alive and well, always creates new music, new poetry, new books, architecture, and new art that celebrate faith. It has also, in different times and spaces recognised that beauty by itself, no matter who created it, somehow reflected something of God's coming reign. Of course the tradition also has its iconoclasm, particularly of the early Protestant kind, yet this same Protestantism rendered Bach, and some of the most inspiring painters of all time!

There is an integral connection between beauty and the journey of justice described above. One of the most telling examples of this comes from the time of the civil rights movement in the United States. Today many former black participants in protest marches in the South recall that the energy and strength to continue was fed at night when the bruised and battered protesters would gather in church and draw on the strength and beauty of Negro Spirituals.[38] These same spirituals were the songs of the oppressed and suffering slaves. Such beauty was created in the midst of the darkest experiences possible. It is this kind of beauty that reflects the coming reign of God. The glorious vision of "Crossing over the Jordan" sustained many in their suffering and enthused other slaves with hope to join the "underground railroad" (the secret routes) to escape to the Northern States and Canada. The kind of beauty that represents the reign of God finds a home in its power that allows people to be inspired and transformed to continue on the journey with hope and joy. It is by no means only present in intentional church liturgy, but it is certainly to be there in song, in dance, in picture, in praise, in music, and in beautiful and moving words.

The practice of beauty in the face of injustice, hopelessness and suffering is a sign of the coming reign of God – it is a sign of hope. It is action derived from the age to come in defiance of the present age and its cynical self-interest.

That is why, when a funeral of a victim of the system was conducted during the apartheid era in South Africa, the gathering of people would throng to a massive event where the raising of voices in the beautiful harmony of traditional Christian hymnody would declare defiance of the power of the present government. Soldiers would stand by, powerless to snuff out such beauty, sometimes they were even overcome by its sheer power.

The renewal of the mind decreed by Paul in Romans 12 surely includes the creation of beauty in all forms of art that expresses the age to come already present and enacted. The practice of beauty – the creation of new work – is not an optional extra when other human needs are met. It is the action of the age to come expressing, celebrating, hymning hope and faith despite all other signs to the contrary. It is, to use Luther's favourite phrase acting *"trotz"* despite or against the evil of this age. Practicing beauty on the journey proclaims how things will be and already are becoming. Perhaps, when Paul breaks out in a hymn of awesome praise to God before he starts Romans 12 he is expressing exactly this idea of beauty that is captured most powerfully in the beauty of the contemplation of the mystery of God (See Romans 11:33-36). Formation for Christian spirituality neglects the encouragement of creative activity at the peril of hope.

The Constructive Journey of Gospel Witness

There is no following of Jesus the Messiah without witness to the Good News for the poor, broken hearted, and marginalised. Evangelism, the bringing of the Good News of the Kingdom, is not an optional extra for special "evangelists" trained in manipulative techniques of mass hypnosis or guilt trips. Evangelism, as Bryan Stone so eloquently argues, is a *practice* of the whole Christian community.[39] He draws here on the arguments of Hütter, Hauerwas, and the moral philosophy of MacIntyre and relates the concept *practice* to the use of the concept *habitus*.

We can conclude that building for the reign of God is a journey of witness to the coming kingdom that grows out of a community on a journey – it is an integral practice of a whole community together. Certainly, there are some with extraordinary gifts of making the Gospel clear to others, who can be specifically called evangelists. But, the journey of formation for Christian spirituality is one that forms all for the communal task of witnessing for the Gospel of the reign of God together.

Elsewhere I have argued that evangelism finds it heart in Genesis 3 when God calls humankind back to communion with the great and passionate cry "Where?" (see also Chapter 1). Our role and place is to bear witness through proclamation and deed to God's call and to embody our response, this we can call evangelism. Without voicing the call to others there is no evangelism, without embodying it in our own response of following Jesus the Messiah there is no substance to evangelism. From the earliest times Christians have spoken about being witnesses to God's coming reign and making the invitation to return or respond to God's cry that we call repentance.

For example, we can return to Acts 1:8 where Luke describes the commissioning of the disciples to become witnesses (*martures*) from which we eventually derived our English word martyr. The bearing of costly witness is an integral part of the journey of the age to come in defiance of the present age. Evangelism as costly witness is therefore an eschatological act in which we bring and enact the Good News of the coming reign of God. Embodying our response means binding up the broken hearted and blessing the poor as well as proclaiming the invitation to follow Jesus the Messiah and to become part of the community of faith. The journey for building the reign of God is inextricably linked to these actions that bring the Good News and carry hope. It is also inextricably linked to the community of faith in which those who respond join the witness of God's coming reign. The journey of formation for Christian spirituality grows integrally out of the journey of evangelism. In the twentieth century we can cite some important examples of people who have demonstrated extraordinary Christian spiritual virtue on the journey.

Sundar Clarke, former Bishop of Madras, tells the story about Bishop Lesslie Newbigin during his time in India embodying this kind of witness. He writes,

> There had been heavy rains which had destroyed a number of houses, huts and school buildings. Without delay Lesslie rushed to these spots and found roofless schools and stunned, apathetic people. He called for a ladder, climbed it, asked the local people to pass him the leaves that had blown off, and began to thatch a shed to make into a school. It was a fascinating spectacle to see him so involved and exhibiting his faith... [40]

In South Africa the witness of Bishop Tutu demonstrates a costly and courageous witness to the Gospel that became transformative in society in community. Who would have dreamt that the power of the Gospel through such leadership would keep that country from becoming a blood bath of revenge? Yet, that is exactly what happened through the work of peace and forgiveness and eventually through the excruciating process of the Truth and Reconciliation

Commission led by Bishop Tutu. In Korea Ahn, Byung Mu and the sisters of the protestant monastic movement *Diakonia Sisterhood* gathered to move into the poorest parts of the city of Seoul to care for the poor[41]. Evangelism defies conventional thinking and invades the present age with the coming reign of God. Evangelism is indeed inviting people to follow Jesus the Messiah, but it grows out of the hope and demonstration of the coming reign of God itself.

Having identified these three kingdom dimensions of the journey of formation – justice, beauty, and witness – we need to continue here to wrestle with the limits of our own role in formation. We also need to understand the core task of practicing discernment.

The Journey of Discernment

In the humble task of formation for Christian spirituality we acknowledge that there is no way that one person or one system can form another for openness on the journey described so far in this chapter. The best we can hope for is to grasp that formation is a matter of witness, leadership and accompaniment. There is no "technology of formation" or a "mastery of the art of formation". Openness can be learned only by the individual self and authenticity can only be lived in the ever challenging journey of participation and being as self. Engaging this journey is a fruit of the work of the Spirit of the Messiah in us, and can only come to fruition when we allow it to grasp us. In terms of the description of the fruit of the Spirit in the Epistles we can say that meekness, longsuffering, gentleness and faith (Gal 5:22-23) all make up dimensions of the openness that we need on the journey. For those who walk with those being formed and the community around them, the task is to encourage this fruit and to discern if it is indeed there. All these qualities are defined by Jesus' steely resolve and unflinching grace in the face of violent opposition.

Evaluation and discernment are critical components of formation for Christian spirituality. Discernment is a profound theological process of the Christian community. It cannot be engaged lightly or frivolously. Neither can we hide behind vague generalisations when we discern. Discernment must have integrity, it must be concrete and the person subject to discernment deserves to know the basis for the discernment. Discernment without respect is not Christian discernment. Respect is shown in discernment by being open and clear about what the concerns are that are being voiced and where problems are identified. It also means that we should be clear with those on the journey what it is that we need to be able to see and experience from them to be able to encourage them further on the way. Respect means that a person is always spoken to in the same way as that person is spoken of when not present. Discernment is a function of community. Because Christian spirituality is lived out and engaged on a journey in community it requires the discerning and guiding presence of others.

Discernment was taken very seriously in the early Christian communities. Even in the band of Jesus' disciples it eventually became clear that Judas' role was discerned as not being on the journey of discipleship. The Book of Acts describes the process of discernment of leadership being engaged with fasting and prayer (Acts 13:2 & 14:23). In each case, and through history, the community of faith played and important role in the process of discernment of vocation. In chapter 1 we saw that not all early Christian leaders were immediately willing to serve even when the community chose to nominate them. For them there often was a struggle with their own willingness to be in a role of leadership. Within the monastic tradition there is a journey of discernment with progress through stages of preparation and commitment. In Protestant Reformed communities the call of the individual always requires the affirmation and support of the community of faith. All have a vocation, some, however, are called to serve and lead the community in a particular way.

Gauging openness on the journey is a necessary part of the process of discernment in formation for Christian spirituality. The best place to do this discernment is not in a theoretical space only, but on the way, in community with fellow learners and in engagement with new and challenging situations. Of course discernment is a spiritual activity (prayer and fasting), but it is rooted in concrete activity and the display of a willingness and openness to learn, to be challenged, to meet and lead others with respect and love. These characteristics, or to use biblical language, these fruits, can be concretely observed and described.

When we engage the journey of Christian spirituality we open ourselves consciously to the discerning function of our community. I suggest here that the rubrics of discernment and evaluation must be rooted in the habits in community described in chapter 2 combined with the dimension of the journey outlined in this chapter. We may begin by discerning habits of community by posing the following questions. After each question we need to reflect on how we would concretely observe the commitment being discerned. First we should ask ourselves these questions and then we can consciously seek the input of others in the community on these same themes.

Questions of Discernment:

We have to ask. Does the person wrestle with **covenant faithfulness** in welcoming the stranger and witnessing to God's plan through Abraham and his family (Israel) for all peoples and the whole world?

Discerning covenant faithfulness thus identifies acts that display a journey that seeks to be hospitable and show respect for others and witness to the Gospel in word and action.

Does the person wrestle with the task of living in this world from the **eschatological** perspective of the world to come engaging others and the cosmos with a commitment to justice in love service and care for the bringing together of all things? Does the person strive to go ahead of others on this way and to invite them along?

Discerning the journey in eschatological hope identifies acts of doing justice in the Spirit of love for humankind and creation. Such eschatological journey is also shown in acts of beauty – creative art, music, and worship that speaks of the world to come. For discerning a call to leadership initiative to lead and encourage others is also part of such a person's life.

Does the person strive to become a **self-giving living sacrifice in love** (mortification) in giving self in loving companionship to others, particularly those who are on the margins? *On the other hand, loving self-giving sacrifice for those on the margins means to live courageously in defiance and in oppositions to the powers of oppression. Courageous and active resistance is an essential part of self-giving.*

Discerning the giving of self to be a part of is shown particularly in acts that show that the person is moving beyond a focus on their own needs only to a focus on the need of those most disadvantaged in their community and the whole world.

Does the person study and learn and act in ways that is on a journey of **transformation**, living out of the resurrection of Jesus the Messiah (vivification) that shows that the person participates in community and seeks to live authentically as self?

Discerning transformation – the renewal of the mind – is done by identifying acts that display change and growth in the person in self-awareness, and awareness of their impact on others. It is also powerfully manifested through the resistance and activism of those marginalised against the oppressor and oppressive systems.

Is the person engaged in the disciplines of learning/studying and **worship in community**?

Discerning this element of growth and change involves evaluating progress in studying Scripture and Tradition and engaging this learning in the context of leadership in worship in community.

Does the person **embody** what they say they believe in the relationships of everyday life?

Discerning embodiment of faith is present in all the acts outlined above and below. It means that one looks not only for words and promises but also for actions.

Does the person, even though imperfect, seek the perfection to which we are invited in following Jesus the Messiah by making an effort in **mission** under the reign of God towards the other, nations, and the cosmos?

We discern a commitment to mission in a person's willingness to be open to and to reach out to people of cultures and socio-economic state different from their own and from observing action for the wholeness of the earth.

These rubrics formulate the dispositions and habits of the spiritual journey of one who is called and grasped by God. They are never perfectly engaged but their shadows are present where the Spirit of the Messiah is at work. A careful analysis of these rubrics will show that the elements of the journey explored above are all present. The journey to the other, the nations, the cosmos, acts of justice, beauty and evangelism are all included. Faith communities that understand their role in formation for Christian spirituality will understand their responsibility to nurture these dispositions, to witness to them by action, and to encourage those who find themselves called and sent. In fact, only when all participating in the community understand themselves as being a part of these dispositions can they fulfill their task of the spiritual journey in example and discernment with faithfulness.

What we do not have explicitly in the journey and discernment description above is a clear link with the traditional disciplines of Christian spirituality. It is to the spirituality of the reign of God that we will turn briefly now, and more fully in chapter 4.

To Conclude: The Spirituality of the Coming Reign of God

David Bosch has described the spirituality of the coming reign of God as a "spirituality of the road."[42] The argument above for the importance of the spiritual journey and its creation-affirming dimensions is a way of working out this idea of an engaged dynamic spirituality. In the previous chapter we referred to the importance of Benedictine spirituality. This important tradition needs to be clearly related to our discussion of journey spirituality and its formative dimensions. The rubrics of prayer and work (*ora et labora*) capture the broad framework of the spirituality of Christian life and formation. In the next chapter we will explore more fully what this means for formation for Christian spirituality. For now it is important to note that work and prayer, as two movements of spiritual activity, make up the warp and woof of the work of the Spirit of the Messiah along our journey. I will argue in the next chapter that these two movements must be understood in the larger context of sacrament. The spirituality of the reign of God points to a constant process of turning in the right direction on the journey. The course corrections are fed by work and prayer that can be unpacked in terms of the Benedictine habits of participating in the sacraments, the study of the Scriptures, worship inspired by the Psalms, prayer as intercession and prayer as action, the practice of being different (holiness) and the practice of love (engaging the other, the nations and the cosmos in acts of hope). All these dimensions of reign of God spirituality can be placed under the heading sacrament. It is to sacrament on the journey that we now turn.

Notes

1. Kearney, R. *The God who May Be*. Bloomington: Indianna University Press, 2001, 52.

2. Bevans, S.B. & Schroeder, R.P. *Constants in Context: A theology of Mission for Today*. New York: Orbis, 2004, 121.

3. Milavic, A. *The Didache: Text, Translation, Analysis and Commentary*. Collegeville: Liturgical Press, 2003.

4. Von Allemn, D. "The Birth of Theology: Contextualization as the Dynamic Element in the Formation of New Testament Theology." in *The International Review of Mission*. 44:253, 1975, pp.37-55.

5. 1 Peter 2:11 Good News Bible.

6. "Thin place" is the Celtic terminology for a place where God is experiences in an intense way.

7. Isaiah 60:17 Good News Bible

8. Karl Barth, *Church Dogmatics III: The Doctrine of Creation 2* Edinburgh: T & T Clark, 1960. 41.

9. This observation does not negate the extreme importance of Nietsche's critique of Western middle class theism and its implications. It simply observes that Nietsche's response leads to either complete despair or to totalitarian authoritarianism.

10. Ibid., 58.

11. Tillich, P. *The Courage to Be*. New Haven: Yale University Press, 1952, 178.

12. The tradition of understanding sin as causing alienation is a long and honourable one that covers the span of Christian tradition from Athanasius through John Calvin and Kierkegaard to Paul Tillich.

13. See Wright's full argument at, Wright, N.T. *Justification* Downers Grove: Intervarsity Press, 2009, 182-201.

14. See for example his comment on Barth in which he claims that Barth reduces all theology to an enlarged doctrine of the "Word of God." Tillich, P. *Systematic Theology. Volume 1. Reason and Revelation, Being and God* (Chicago: Chicago University Press, 1951) 122. For Tillich the personal encounter with God, so important in Judaeo-Christian tradition, is only an inadequate part of revelation.

15. Tillich, P. *The Courage to Be*. Ibid., 190.

16. For example, Tillich makes this assertion about "absolute faith", as "a movement in with and under other states of mind." In this regard, although I might not agree with his definition of "absolute faith", I do agree with his understanding of the dynamic nature of our ongoing process of becoming ourselves as acts of courage. However, encounter can remain dynamic, in fact it is so if it is understood as an ongoing journey towards our most vulnerable neighbours. See, Tillich, Ibid. 188.

17. Ibid., 86-154.

18. Levinas, Emmanuel *On Thinking-of-the-Other Entre Nous* (Translated Smith, M.B. & Harshaw, B.) New York: Columbia University, 1998. p. 110.

19. Tillich, *Systematic Theology: Volume 1.* Ibid., 113.

20. Tillich, *The Courage to Be,* Ibid., 106-107.

21. Ibid., 110.

22. Ibid., 188.

23. Wright, N.T. *Surprised by Hope: Rethinking Heaven, the Resurrection, and the Mission of the Church.* (New York: Harper One, 2008), 236.

24. Ibid., 241.

25. See Terence Fretheim insightful discussion of Genesis 2:5-17 and particularly his unpacking of the meaning of *'abad* (to serve) and *šāmar* (to keep, protect) in Gen. 2:15. *God and the World in the Old Testament: A Relational Theology of Creation.* Nashville: Abingdon Press, 2005. 53-54.

26. "White Monastery" refers to the idea of "white martyrdom" or willing self-giving sacrifice for the sake of the Gospel. Such monastic life prepared people to travel sacrificially for the Gospel.

27. Bosch, Ibid. 489.

28. Levinson, D. J. *The Seasons of a Man's Life.* New York: Random House, 1978.

29. Gilligan, C. *In A Different Voice: Psychological Theory and Women's Development.* Harvard: Harvard University Press, 1982.

30. Some examples of post-colonial authors are Homi K. Bhabha, Gayati C. Spivak and Edmund Said.

31. Wright, Ibid., 208.

32. See Bosch Ibid., 70-73

33. Bosch, Ibid., 71.

34. Ibid.

35. Ibid., 72.

36. Ibid., 72-73.

37. Wright, Ibid. 222.

38. See the PBS series, *Thus Far by Faith.*

39. Stone, B. *Evangelism after Christendom: The Theology and Practice of Christian Witness.* Grand Rapids: Brazos Press, 2007.

40. Clarke cited in Goheen, M. *As the Father Has Sent Me, I Am Sending You":J. E. Lesslie Newbigin's Missionary Ecclesiology* Utrecht: Die Boekencentrum, 2000, 249.

41. See http://www.shinsonhapkido.ch/db_isha/aktuell_isha/dateien_aktuell/42b67ed561c61.pdf acessed August 1, 2011.

42. Bosch, D.J. *A Spirituality of the Road.* Eugene: Wipf and Stock, 2001.

4

Sacrament

The multitude of stars is received by Abraham as a sign of the power of God in his life. The sign is not proof or demonstration, but it is a sacrament to those who can discern the connection between the concrete visible and the promised... The new pilgrimage of Abraham is not grounded in the old flesh of Sarah nor the tired bones of Abraham, but in the disclosing word of God.[1]

We do not deal here first with the sacraments of the church, although we shall come back to them later, but rather with the general idea of sacrament as Breuggemann intends it in the quotation above. Abraham's journey is launched in the sign of the mystery of the multitude of the stars that Abraham takes as a sign of God awe inspiring promise that he will become the father of many nations. Every journey of formation is a journey of hope supported by the sacramental promise of God and sacramental signs that calls and sustains us on the journey. We have noted that David Bosch coined the title "a spirituality of the road." Because the road speaks of the earthy, dusty, embodied living of our spirituality on the road of very day, we can say that this title speaks well to the idea of sacrament, the visible – the sign of what is to come. The spirituality of the road therefore speaks of the idea of walking the way of spirituality in sacramental obedience. In this chapter I will use the descriptor "spirituality of the road" to emphasise the embodied and sacramental nature of Christian spirituality. We hear the call, we listen, and we journey in the habits of Christian spirituality. To sustain us on this journey God gives us **sacrament**. Like Abraham we stand in need of sacrament to help us continue the journey of Christian spirituality.

In his thought-provoking book, *The Creative Word: Canon as a Model for Biblical Education*, Breuggemann argued that there are four dimensions to the canonical structure of biblical education and formation.[2] For those to whom this language is new, "canon" refers to the idea of the Bible as measure of our faith. Breuggemann identifies the following four dimensions:

1. The disclosure of binding (law) (focused on the giving of the Torah)
2. The disruption for justice (grounded in the challenge of the prophets)
3. The discernment of order (built from the wisdom literature in the Bible)
4. Obedience as mode of knowledge (based in the message of the Psalms)

The structure of this book also attempts to reflect these dimensions. The disclosure of binding is represented in the first two chapters with emphasis on call, limitation, freedom, and listening. The disruption of justice is rooted in chapter three which focuses on the journey character of formation including mortification, the journey to the other and the cosmos. Discernment of order belongs in the large picture painted together of how all the aspect of our meaning on earth fits into God's creative work. The task of obedience will be engaged in this chapter and the next as we examine sacrament and mission. It is the fourth dimension – obedience – that brings the other three in creative tension and it is to the story of obedience to God that we now turn as we explore the spirituality of formation. Obedience will also lead us to another insight into our theological understanding of human anthropology. It is captured in Rabbi Abraham Heschel's famous conclusion, "I am commanded therefore I am."[3] We will explore the sacramental journey of the spirituality of the road in terms of the two parts of Benedictine spirituality, prayer (ora) and work (labora).

Before we continue we need to remind ourselves of the meaning of the concept sacrament. The Latin word sacramentum was the translation of the Greek word mysterion which appears in the New Testament (see for example Col. 1:26) associated with the Gospel story of the incarnation, life, death and resurrection of Jesus. This word mysterion indicates a great secret or mystery now concretely revealed in Jesus Christ. Thus in a real way the most basic sacrament is the appearance of God in human form in creation. This is a visible sign of God's grace for us. Sacrament therefore became associated with the idea of visible signs in our world of the invisible grace of God associated with Jesus the Messiah. If we speak here of sacrament we mean it in the wide sense that indicates the signs God gives us of God's faithful loving grace to encourage and sustain us on the journey. All these signs in some way relate to Jesus the Messiah himself and the story of his appearance.

First we turn to Prayer as a physical activity that reminds us and ensures us of God's loving grace.

The Journey of Prayer – Ora

Breuggemann observes that in the Psalms God is addressed as "Thou". This stance in the Psalms enlightens prayer and its meaning on a very basic level. He observes,

> First, to say "Thou" requires a deep and concrete faith in God. One cannot speak a "Thou" into and empty sky. Second, if one is fixed on the self, the utterance of "Thou" is a dangerous diminishment, a violation of my self as ultimate concern.[4]

The Hebrew "Thou" in the Psalms does not disappear in pious grovelling, but includes bitter lament as well as rapturous praise. It dances with nature, but always with nature as creation of God sustained by God's love and presence, never with nature as God-self. It is not particularly mystical, but it is lyrical in beautiful poetry and always firmly grounded in the ethics of relational account-ability. The Psalms play a key role in the prayer cycle of the rule of Saint Bene-dict.[5] This tradition was also absorbed into various protestant traditions. So, for example, the reading of a Psalm in public worship makes up a very impor-tant part of both Anglican and Reformed tradition, and this is even augmented with the tradition to sing a Psalm as the opening hymn of worship. The Psalms as prayers thus formed both the model and the core of prayer spirituality within the Christian church from very early times on.

Even though the Psalms affirm our human emotions of despair, anger at God, and struggle with suffering, they always bring us back to acknowledging the importance of the "Thou" of God as the one to obey. Breuggemann con-cludes, "Communion with the God of Israel is understood primarily in terms of obedience."[6] This means that prayer is always an ethical event and cannot be mystified away from God and neighbour. Prayer as depicted in the Psalms is a journey that leads us through our difficult emotions and questions, but it always ends in obedience linked to God, neighbour and community.

There are of course elements in the Psalms that pose big problems for the ethic of the Christian faith. The partisan celebration of the killing of ene-mies and children is not something we should associate with prayer (see Psalm 137:9). We need to understand these dimensions of the Psalms in the con-text of the difficult journey of a desperate struggle for survival of a people and against the greater structure of the Decalogue in the Torah that unequivocal-ly say, "You shall not kill." We also need to understand such outbursts in the Psalms as part of the human process of the psychological journey from anger, revenge, and hatred to obedience to God as the "Thou" that relativises our own pain and suffering. There is therefore a therapeutic element to the Psalms and to the logic of Christian prayer.

Prayer as the Journey to Obedience

> Listen, O my son, to the precepts of thy master, and incline the ear of thy heart, and cheerfully receive and faithfully execute the admonitions of thy loving Father, that by the toil of obedience thou mayest return to Him from whom by the sloth of disobedience thou hast gone away. (Prologue to the Rule of Saint Benedict)

It is therefore no surprise that Benedictine spirituality has no qualms about counselling obedience. However, the rule is clear that obedience is not something we are truly able to do by our own effort alone, but it is in the first place something received by grace from God.[7] In fact, the prayer for obedience is one of the key instructions of Saint Benedict. The Rule of Saint Benedict clearly emphasises the prevenience of God's grace so important to all Christian traditions[8].

Even though obedience, placed in its context in the Rule, deals with obedience to the Abbot and the hierarchical structure of that kind of monastery, it is clear that the principle behind obedience is obedience to God and even obedience to the Abbot as leader is premised on the Abbot's obedience to God. Prayer as the journey to obedience, the love of God, and neighbour therefore is the heart of a spirituality of the road and the spirituality steeped in the Psalms. Prayer therefore strengthens the habit of **covenant faithfulness.**

Prayer as Eschatological Journey

As I write this chapter I have just listened to an interview with an Atheist reporter who spent a considerable time in the Middle East and in the Iraq war. He expressed his shock at the depth of credulity that faith has reached in some fundamentalist groups on all sides of the divide. When asked if he prayed when in true danger during the Iraq war he said that he did, but more as an expression of firm emotion that he will survive than in an expectation of God intervening on his behalf. Prayer can easily be reduced to such a psychological level in our present culture where the verbal expression "O my God" has become one of the most trivial expressions around. Prayer, however, both in the Psalms and in the Lord's Prayer takes on a dimension of pregnant and dynamic intercession in expectation. In the light of the Christian hope, born out of the resurrection of Jesus the Messiah, prayer takes on as an essential element this eager expectation and sighs for what is to come. In Jesus' prayer this is expressed in the words, "Let your kingdom come." In Romans Paul describes this eschatological intercession thus,

> Yet there was the hope that creation itself would one day be set free from its slavery to decay and would share the glorious freedom of the children of God. For we know that up to the present time all of creation groans with pain, like the pain of childbirth. But it is not just creation alone which groans; we who have the Spirit as the first of God's gifts also groan within ourselves as we wait for God to make us his children and set our whole being free. (Romans 8:20-28, GNB)

I cite this passage because it is fundamental to the spirituality of the road. Spirituality for Christian leadership can only grow out of the travail of prayer and sighing for the coming reign of God and carried on the wings of the Spirit of the Messiah at work within us. Here we are reminded that in a very real way the Christian journey is a journey of prayer in the Spirit. We who open ourselves to the Spirit are not yet complete, we wait to be made into God's children – we are on a journey of prayerful hopeful waiting and doing. All of this conception of the coming of redemption and the journey of God's reign is pulled forward by the deep conviction in hope that, "creation itself would one day be set free from its slavery to decay and would share the glorious freedom of the children of God." Such prayer enthused with eschatological expectation, intercession, and hope carries the spirit of the Christian life and the strength to engage the journey towards God, neighbour and the sighing and groaning creation.

Prayer is a physical activity. It occurs in our bodies and involves our feelings, bodies, and mind. We can engage prayer individually, but never individualistically. For when we pray we stand always in relationship with others, we pray for others and we pray before God. Prayer is not escape, it is engagement, it fulfills a vital sacramental role that strengthens us on the journey of spirituality.

Prayer as The Journey in Awe

Breuggemann writes,

> ...we deal with a mystery, a compelling mystery, but a mystery whose name we know, so that we call this one "Thou."[9]

And, Saint Benedict,

> Let us then rise at length, since the Scripture arouseth us, saying: "It is now the hour for us to rise from sleep" (Rom 13:11); and having opened our eyes to the deifying light, let us hear with awestruck ears what the divine voice, crying out daily, doth admonish us, saying: "Today, if you shall hear his voice, harden not your hearts" (Ps 94[95]:8). (From the Prologue of the Rule of Saint Benedict)

If we take seriously that the Psalms address God as "Thou" and that this "Thou" is not derived from "I", then prayer, can never be something folksy that seeks to domesticate God. Much popular Christian spirituality in North America goes that way. God or Jesus is made into a pal to chat up rather than the fearsome struggle with our emotions of anger, joy and pain before the "Thou" that addresses us and calls us into being. If God came to earth in Jesus the Messiah, and if Jesus came to identify with our humanity, it does not follow that Jesus the Messiah is now domesticated into our house idol. He is the coming eschatological judge, before him every knee shall bow and every tongue confess, he is the one who calls us to costly discipleship. There is absolutely no room for folksiness in public Christian prayer. There is room for anger, lament, and pain, but always in the presence of the "Thou" we encounter as God and who calls us to obedience. Christian prayer, whether public or private, always moves on the journey of awe before the "Thou" who is God. This sense of awe in prayer is another element of Benedictine spirituality steeped in the Psalms. As we have seen in the previous chapter, we encounter God in and through the neighbour, but we also encounter God as being far more than that – beyond the human condition. The humanity of Jesus the Messiah does not exhaust his Divinity.

For those on the journey of formation for Christian leadership prayer in awe has to be a key part of our journey. Prayer that diminishes and domesticates God does not reflect the Spirit of the Messiah and will fail us in the tough task that lies ahead. Only where we can pray in awe and honesty, without false piety, will we find the strength that is brought by the vision and the power of communion with God that drinks from the well of obedience. One does not obey a pal, but you do obey when addressed by the awesome presence of the "Thou" of God. Of course, such an awe inspired relationship in prayer does not preclude intimacy and should not keep us in our private prayers from expressing intimate love for God and our Lord Jesus Christ. However, at all times the respect of awe is part of that intimacy.

The Journey of Sacrament as Prayer and Prayer as Sacrament

It was in part my own stupidity. I left my residence room unlocked and this allowed the Methodist Chaplain, Vic Pearce, at the University in Cape Town to march into my room at 6 am to invite me to early morning Eucharist at the Anglican Bishop's home. At 18 I had never set foot in an Anglican Church and was not really all that interested in doing so at 6 am in the morning. Because of the haze of the previous night's pub-crawl I found myself in the Chaplain's car in a dirty T-shirt and jeans together with 4 other students not quite knowing how I got there. The Eucharist was held in a small chapel on the side of the Bishop's house. I tried to stay ahead of the kneeling and standing, and thumping through prayer books all quite unfamiliar to me, when the bishop suddenly stopped procedure. He cleared his throat and suggested that because there were only a few of us present we could spend some time in prayer before we moved on to sharing the Eucharist. Then it happened. A black woman seated across from me started to pray with great earnestness for the students at the university and particularly those who were present. She prayed for us to have strength to resist temptations (the pub crawl the previous night painfully came to my mind), and she prayed God's blessing on our hard work and study (my lack of academic effort played graphically before me...). At that point in my life, as a South African white boy, I had never actually touched a black person. It just never came up as a possibility. But the bishop proceeded to invite us to share the peace before the Eucharist and the black woman made a b-line for me across the chapel. She wrapped me in her arms and held me in a tight hug and she whispered, "the peace of the Lord be with you." I knew then as I know now that God had wrapped me in a warm embrace through that woman. It was both the embrace of judgement and the embrace of liberation. Judgement descended in exposing my deep racial prejudice, liberation came in the love that would not let me go. The bread and the wine were signs of the judging saving work of God. Sacrament was prayer and prayer was sacrament.

As sure as Abraham in prayerful awe before God saw the expanse of the stars as the assurance of God's promise that he will have a son and that in him all nations would be blessed, so sure did that prayer filled and ethically charged sacramental moment bring a conviction of hope to my racist and traitorous heart that morning. It was another step on a journey of prayer that will not let me forget my neighbour and my responsibility to them.

Prayer and the sacraments of the church are of course integrally linked. This is true whether we follow the Protestant focus on Baptism and Eucharist as the core sacraments, or if we include also the seven sacraments of the Roman Catholic tradition. Either way, we can never separate the sacraments from prayer. All that we have said above goes for prayer in the context of sacrament.

We can see this prayer-sacrament phenomenon dramatically expressed in Baptism. Baptism is a prayer for repentance, an act of obedience, a sign of God's coming reign, and is practiced vows in utmost awe and wonder before God. Baptism is repentance enacted and demonstrated. It is the work of the sighing and groaning of the Spirit expressed in action. It is witness and humility wrapped in the movements of mortification (dying under the waters) and vivification (rising with the Messiah). In fact, even if the act of Baptism were not to include any words, its very enactment would be a sign and a prayer. Moreover, baptism is entrance into a new community bringing together the newly baptised and the community of faith in a new and dramatic relationship. Baptism is thus prayer embodied.

My story above links the Eucharist and prayer in similar ways. The journey of prayer is to be a Eucharistic one. Obedience to the Messiah's command "do this in remembrance of me", the awe of sharing the elements, the great prayer of thanksgiving linking together the church throughout the ages and the church throughout the world, the eschatological hope that ends with the traditional cry, Maranatha – "Come Lord Jesus!", all express sacrament as prayer. It also draws us into a community of ethical accountability. Not only does the Pauline tradition point out that rich and poor should be united at the table without exploitation, but John Calvin pointed out that there is not true sacrament while we leave our neighbour in the gutter.[10]

Prayer in its own way has a sacramental dimension. When engaged publicly and in groups, the experience of prayer and the words of praying neighbours give substance to hope. It may become a sign that allows us to trust God and to act against the cynical and jaded attitudes of our time. When engaged in honesty and awe before God who is "Thou", prayer expresses faith in an embodied shape.

The Journey of Prayer as Study

For a book on formation for Christian spirituality I have said little about the discipline of the mind. This might seem peculiar for a Presbyterian who is part of a tradition that prides itself (not always with good substance) in its empha-

sis on academic education! Study, particularly the study of the Scriptures, theology, and the Christian tradition, can perhaps also be placed in the context
of the Benedictine principle of work. However, I deliberately place it in the
context of prayer. There are many ways of studying theology and the Bible.
My concern here is not to critique these different approaches, but to argue that
the study of the Scriptures, theology and Christian tradition, for those being
formed on the journey for Christian spirituality should proceed from the place
of prayer. The forming of our minds in the light of God's call and the understanding evoked in the loving study of Scripture and tradition is an act of worship, its practice *is* doxology.

Things are completely dynamic in our present world and we live in a context of break-neck change. This means that study needs new ways of function-
ing in our situation. In a moment of unusual frankness a retiring colleague told
me some years ago, "I have learned how to lead people in worship and how to
help them survive as Christians in the secularising Canadian society. What I
have not learned and have no idea about is how to lead them with faith into the
future they face." He was, until his retirement serving a worshipping community that was surviving though slowly dwindling and he felt ill prepared to deal
with this challenge. All he knew to do was to work harder at what he knew
to do. What he did not know is how to face the constant state of change, disruption, and cynical challenge that his community and his own ministry coun-
tenanced. He did not know how to journey as a sojourner from the world to
come in this present age.

It is my contention here that living on the journey of Christian spirituality
into the present age, which has become the future-present technological age in
our North American context, requires a new rooting in eschatological prayer
and sacrament through disciplined study. As Luther insisted that one needed to
act "*trotz*" against and despite the present age, so too, our formation in study
should help those being formed to live out of the strength of the sighing and
groaning Spirit of the Messiah who will lead us through as we struggle against
the current.

I have made a case elsewhere to identify the heart of the challenge before
the North American church in the quest for mastery over creation and ultimately God.[11] This challenge does not come to us only in the shape of "secular culture" it comes to us more subversively in the shape of the "successful church".
The successful church in the North American context is often described as "missional" not denoting the costly journey of discipleship under the cross – the real
meaning of "missional church", but rather the triumphal propagation of itself in
drawing increasing numbers of people into its fold. It measures with the mea-

sure of the world: impressive numbers, productive programs, financial buoy-
ancy, and impressive buildings. It manipulates by means of technology for its
own ends and it does so in the name of a god that it identifies with Jesus. In
its most extreme forms its gospel is prosperity and its salvation is wealth. But
in its most misleading form it is not quite so boldly heretical, it is rather heretical in misdirection rather than direction. It wraps itself in the cloak of claiming
cultural relevance but does so without seeking obedience when that relevance
does not reflect the signs of the age to come. Study, particularly the study of
Christian history and tradition, will help us understand that these temptations
have always been around in slightly different shapes throughout Christian history. Study of the Scriptures will help us discern where the way of Jesus Christ,
the way of the self-giving sacrifice in love, the cruciform way is different from
these commercial and consumer models of church.

The only way to counter such an alluring spirit is through the constant
journey and habit of prayerful study before God who is our "Thou" as outlined
above. When we study Scripture, theology and tradition, we must thus start
with prayer. Not prayers as a piousness that shirks the hard questions, but
prayer as hope against the power and allure of a success based production culture with its quick fixes. To return again to Paul Tillich's analysis discussed in
Chapter 3, what we face is the merging of North American production democracy with a pseudo death-and-suffering-denying belief in "life after death" that
feeds a kind of consumer-culture-Christianity far removed from the world
challenging and changing faith of the coming Messiah.

The confusion of the culture of the present age and its consumer goods
with faith was most powerfully demonstrated to me at a conference I attended
some years ago. A speaker of a new alternative church in the "emergent
church" movement was not receiving as hearty an applause for his rousing
speech about embracing technology in church. In frustration he pulled his I-
Phone out of his pocket. "You don't get it." He said. "This is where Christianity is at" as he swung the I-Phone in front of us he said, "If you don't get the
pivotal importance of this I-Phone this generation will pass you by." It is with
such sincere but deeply flawed confusion that we often deal in North America.
In some ways this challenge is much harder than open hostility. Afterwards, in
conversation with a woman who is part of the new Protestant Monastic community committed to the marginalised neighbourhoods in the inner city in the
Southern United States confessed that her little community, does not have a
website or and I-Phone. They do have a community garden, they have neighbours who come for dinner, and they make friends with the homeless and mentally ill. Often they provide a warm place to sleep.

These two contrasting examples illustrate how difficult it is to face the subtle temptations that can only be dealt with in a spirituality that has survived the ages, a Benedictine, prayer soaked, obedience to the Gospel that lives out of the world to come. Such spirituality understands that we are about meeting the "Thou" of God in our neighbour, the marginalised, and in the cosmos itself. Without the sign and sacrament, without prayer in community, without faith rooted in the great habits of Christianity we risk creating a religious sham.

Such prayer then brings us to rigorous study. Study is prayer and prayer is study. This process of study also challenges us today to engage great diversity. This diversity is captured in the journey to the nations, and the journey to the cosmos that we discussed in the previous chapters. It is also rooted in the righteousness-justice of God. Such a prayerful form of study explores the great traditions of Biblical study, theology and tradition while holding them together in obedience to God as "Thou". Such theological study, as Dorothy Soelle argued, is not just "faith seeking to understand" as per Saint Anselm's famous definition, but above all "love seeking to understand".[12] Such love in study is born of true prayer in obedience.

N.T. Wright cites a striking example of such prayer based leadership and spirituality that invaded this world with the world to come. Again, the example is from South Africa. Bishop Desmond Tutu, not someone to let the grass of injustice grow under his feet, is known to spend up to three hours in prayer every morning.[13] As we saw earlier, another example is Bishop Lesslie Newbigin. He was also a man not shy to engage the challenges of justice and the concrete embodiment of the Gospel. He played a pivotal role in establishing the united Church of South India but his action was rooted in prayer. One of his colleagues from the Indian National Council of Churches comments about Newbigin's reputation in Kanchipuram:

> "One spoke about the regular and punctual morning devotions in which he used to sit engrossed in meditation in the mornings on the terrace of the Mission Bungalow, on the Railway Road, till the rays of the sun disturbed him."[14]

Both these people have made a significant impact through study and publication. Desmond Tutu has done so through his many publications reflecting on the challenges of racism, homophobia, and reconciliation, and Newbigin in the editorship of the International Review of Mission, and the writing of many pivotal and influential theological books in the twentieth century. Disciplined prayerful study, particularly of the Scriptures and those who explore them, has a powerful sacramental dimension. It provides a concrete sign of God's grace in the great stories of faith and tradition that instruct and inspire us.

The discipline of prayerful study strengthens the habit of **working hard on the way.**

The Prayerful Journey Towards Wise Knowledge

We live in an environment where information is inflated with a corollary decline in wisdom. Given these realities, how do we contribute to the formation of wisdom on the journey of Christian spirituality? My conclusion is that there is only one response adequate to this question, to ensure that we get exposed to the broad tradition. By broad I mean global not just Western or European perspectives. Yes, we do need to be evaluative and discerning as we read and study, we do need to ask questions, we do need to critically engage both Scripture and tradition, we do need to have new constructive ways of engaging our world and culture, but we cannot do so if we do not know and understand some of the outline of the body of work we call Scripture and traditions. Part of this "old fashioned" conviction is that exposure to such traditions allows us to discover what we do not know and protects us from the mistake of thinking that our constructive ideas are new. Learning the traditions is therefore not an optional extra, but a pivotal part of prayerful obedience on the Christian spiritual journey. This does not mean that we need the sophisticated apparatus of university courses and so on to follow Christian spirituality (although this may be helpful). Even in a small African village Christians can benefit from hearing and reading the Scriptures for themselves and then hear back reflection from someone who has studied further. The West African New Testament Scholar Justin Ukpong described using this process in the person he describes as the "expert reader" with the community[15]. Such study of traditions expresses the virtue of humility by respecting those who have gone before.

Prayerfully Waiting on the Journey

> Blessed are the meek: for they shall inherit the earth (Mt 5:5, GNB)
> But those that wait for Jehovah, they shall inherit the land. (Ps 37:9, ASV)

Every journey involves waiting. The link between the "meek" inheriting the earth (Mt. 5:5) and "those who wait" inheriting the land (Ps. 37:9) is not inconsequential. The juxtaposition of these intimately related texts link waiting-meekness with a disposition before the "Thou" who addresses us in the context of prayer. "Waiting" then does not mean meaningless inaction, but an embodied presence before the "Thou" of God. Waiting occurs in space and time and is material – embodied before God and it grows out of the promise of God's coming gift represented in "the land" or "the earth". This kind of eschatological waiting is prayer.

We can now see how "waiting" is integral to the spirituality of the road. Waiting means action born out of prayer before the "Thou" of God who gifts us with the ability to act. It is perhaps another way to capture Paul's assertion that we work out our salvation with fear and trembling while God is at will and work within us. Waiting expresses the integral link between human action for the reign of God as our effort and human action for the reign of God as God's gift.

Waiting obviously has a temporal dimension. But, one can wait with impatience, frustration, and in hopelessness. This is not the kind of waiting encountered in the spirituality of the road. The spirituality of the road waits in meaningful time, it implies patient waiting ready to act, and active waiting ready to pause. Moreover such waiting stands against the spirit of our age that is a spirit of self-fabrication. Pamela McCarroll describes this beautifully,

> A posture of waiting is particularly subversive in the North American context. Waiting challenges all the ways that the liberal image of the human as creative agent and master has shaped our self-understanding as a continent. In North America, we are 'doers,' we make history and we change the world (we do not wait upon or for it). 'To wait' means we are at the mercy of some o/Other upon whose revealing we wait.[16]

Such prayerful waiting, that Pamela captures with the Biblical metaphor of "the coming of the thief in the night", marks a spirituality of the road for our time.

Waiting is captured in the tradition of Saint Benedict with the rule of silence. Chapter VI of the rule reflects on the dangers of talking too much. It appears rather dour and decries speech for humour or simply for the sake of conversation. Of course, such a take on silence misses speech as a gift of the human condition, conversation as the central part of what we know about Jesus' ministry, and speech as expressed in the beauty of literature and poetry. It denies the importance of conversation as an integral part of loving our neighbour. We should defend and recover these important human dimensions of speech even speech as humour and mirth. After all, we know from scholarship today that there is much Hebrew humour in the scriptures! In the New Testament we find Nathanial's humorous retort reported in the Gospel of John.[17] Nevertheless silence as a key element of prayer has become underrated in our sound soaked world. In this Saint Benedict still has something to teach us. Knowing and cultivating appropriate silence, particularly in the space of worship is part of active waiting, listening, and attending to God we encounter as "Thou" in prayer. Waiting and its expression in the discipline of silence is a pivotal dimension of leadership in Christian community and therefore a critical part of formation.

The Journey of Prayerful Praise

I will celebrate, sing unto the Lord,
I will sing to God a new song
I will sing to God a new song
I will praise God, I will sing to God a new song
I will praise God, I will sing to God a new song
Hallelujah, Hallelujah, Hallelujah, Hallelujah, I will sing to God a new song
Hallelujah, Hallelujah, Hallelujah, Hallelujah, I will sing to God a new song
I will celebrate, sing unto the Lord
I will sing to God a new song
I will sing to God a new song[18]

Marva Dawn cites the song above as an example of "praise" devoid of God and full of us. Simply count the number of "I's"! This is perhaps an extreme example empty self-absorption in contemporary "praise songs", but it is symptomatic of a religious culture that has lost its sense of "Thou". After the human struggles with fear, anger, and despair are processed the Psalms culminate in the praise of God as "Thou." The conclusions are consistently that our pain and suffering, though real and relevant, find their resolution in praise. A spirituality of the road that will be able to countenance our time and challenges would thus have to find its culmination in the ongoing work of prayerful praise of God as "Thou". This clear focus on the praise of God as subject, always has content in the Psalms. Praise is never empty of narrative. In the Psalms praise tells the story of God, God's acts, and God's being as discovered in human experience, the stories of God's actions, and in creation. In the opening words of the Lord's Prayer where God's name is worshipped as holy and honoured, is described in terms of God's beyondness denoted by the words "in heaven".

We can see the qualitative difference between the song cited above and most of the church's store of praise hymnody that is brimming with narrative content drawn mainly from the scriptural tradition. Of course, there is much in traditional hymnody that can also be misleading; this is particularly obvious in the shift of 19th century piety where the expectation of the resurrection of the dead is shifted to the vague concept of life after death in heaven.

In chapter 3 we explored the importance of beauty as a sign of leadership for the coming of God's reign. Leadership in prayerful praise is one of the most important places where such beauty is to be practiced. The critique of a contemporary song above is not a critique of the intention of constant new expressions of the praise of God. Where we cease to be creatively new in our praise we lose the ability to respond the constant challenge of the spirit of our own age. New times do require new praise that defies the power of the present age. One example of a great hymn that did just that during the Second World War is Harry Emmerson Fosdick's hymn, *God of Grace and God of glory* that captured the need to counter the warring madness of the 20th century. Fosdick chose a traditional tune, but new music to accompany such praise is also called for. Leadership in prayerful praise will carry the strength of knowing the tradition in creative leadership of meeting and challenging the times we live in. Such leadership will draw on the great well of traditions in worship and will build new ways of celebrating the greatness of God.

The praise of God is represented in the theological tradition with the concept *doxology.* Doxology is one of the great constants of the Christian church. Some of the earliest depictions of Christians are depictions of people with hands raised in prayer and praise to God. Theology itself, where it is practiced for Christian leadership, grows out of such doxology. It is no surprise then that Jürgen Moltmann, in his reflection on his own journey as theologian states, "The place of Christian theology was pre-eminently worship, the doxology of the Triune God."[19] It is exactly where doxology in prayerful praise is present that love can seek to understand God. Doxology, in the formation of Christian leadership is therefore the place where theological learning begins. What we sing is what we truly believe.

So far we have identified the contours of the spirituality of Christian formation as a journey of prayer. This journey of prayer, we have argued is fundamentally sacramental as a sign of God's grace and it includes, obedience, eschatological hope, awe, sacrament, wisdom, study, waiting, and doxological praise. Out of such a spirituality of the road that is a spirituality of *ora* (prayer) grows the person who can journey to the neighbour, the nations, the cosmos, and being as self. Because of the embodied and ethical nature of such a spirituality of the road, it is inseparable from *labora* building for the coming reign of God. It is to the spirituality of the road as work that we now turn.

The habit of **working hard on the way** requires work.

The Spirituality of the Road as labora

Let the brethren serve each other so that no one be excused from the
work in the kitchen, (The Rule of Saint Benedict, Chapter XXXV).

One of the great legacies of the monastic tradition during the medieval period
was its unflinching commitment to ordinary work, planting, and building. We
return here to David Bosch's account of the awe-inspiring power of this commitment. He writes about the resilience of the monastic movement in the face
of repeated destruction and comments,

> Coupled with this was the refusal to write off the world as a lost cause
> or to propose neat, no-loose-ends answers to the problems of life, but
> rather to rebuild promptly, patiently, and cheerfully, "as if it were by
> some law of nature that the restoration came."[20]

The emphasis on the validity of the tasks of everyday is part of the moderation
and beauty of the Benedictine rule. Behind it, however, lies a strength and
tenacity, where work, restoration, and rising to the challenge of decay and destruction was met with unprecedented resilience. The spirituality of the road
for today's Christians requires a recovery of such resilience in action. So much
of the desperate attempts of churches in North America to create activity and
growth by means of technology and manipulation are born out of fear in the
face of a world that seems bent on destruction of faith. To meet this challenge
we must not react out of such desperation and panic. If we do so we simply
give in to the desire to look good to the present age. We need monastic resilience that will go ahead and build and work in faith at the ordinary tasks before us despite all seemingly hopeless news that come our way. When 99 out
of a hundred are taken down, the one that remains, in faithfulness to God's call,
must return and start *labora*. Such action is born from the age to come. Such
action is born out of non-conformity to the measures of the present age. In the
Biblical story the idea of the remnant that remains faithful to God in the face
of great opposition captures this resilience. Such action reflects the habit of **eschatological living.**

By now it should be clear that such resilient work can only grow out of the
spirituality of the road as prayer explored earlier. Fed by the well of prayer, as
did the monastics of old, we too can face our own dark age ahead.

The Spirituality of the Road as a Spirituality that Builds

In chapter 3 we examined N.T. Wright's argument that we are to *build for* the reign of God. This way of describing our human agency tries to capture the truth that God brings God's reign and that our task is a more humble one that builds for it, and with it. We join what God is already at work doing. We work in the capacity of participating in the reign of God rather than bringing it into being. What we build is not equal to God's reign, nor does it exhaust it. What we build will have flaws, but what we build – the *labora* we are called to do – are signs of the coming reign. Such signs are at best sacramental – they are signs that point beyond themselves to God's grace at work.

This idea of sign was developed by Lesslie Newbigin in his Kerr Lectures as Trinity College, Glasgow in 1953. There he argued that the church is to be a sign of God's coming reign, but also a foretaste of the reign to come and the first fruits of the reign of God that has come.[21] In his subsequent work this theme was continued consistently. The three categories of sign, foretaste, and fruit supply the theological framework for the work of Christian spirituality and leadership. We can capture it by describing our work of spirituality as,

1. We journey to build signs of God's coming reign
2. We live in such a way of love and service that we provide a taste of what is to come
3. We grow to bear the fruit of the Spirit of the coming Messiah

It is critical that we understand these work dimensions of the spirituality of the road as dynamic not static. We cannot lose sight of the journey character at this stage of our discussion because it is exactly a spirituality of the *road*. Let us now explore the three dimensions of *labora* along the road of spirituality.

We Journey to Build Signs of God's Coming Reign

Christians always create and build things. Even though the first Christians met in homes and other secret gathering places such as the catacombs in Rome, the practice of building places of worship started very early. Even when Christians hid in the catacombs they decorated their space with works of art. By building, I do not only mean building things, but I mean the general creative activity that reflects God's coming reign. The composition of music, the writing of prose and poetry, the creation of correspondence, the production of theological reflection, the painting of icons and later art, and of course the construction of places of worship all speak of the creative impulse to build in Christian tradition. As we saw with N.T. Wright's argument for beauty as a sign of

God's coming reign in the previous chapter we can acknowledge that all these dimensions together with new media remain signs or witnesses of God's coming reign.

In Chapter 3 we noted how Michael Kearney speaks of this reality as "fragments of stone and story" that are "Ciphers, perhaps, of a transfiguring God."[22] This is another way of saying that these creative works are acts that are signs of God's coming to us and these works stand as witnesses to God breaking into the present world and transforming creation. As I have mentioned before, these signs are not perfect and are not to be confused with a perfect replication of God's reign. So, for example, we can stand in awe of the great Cathedral of Chartres and we can be drawn into the worship of God in such a place, however, such Cathedrals also carry a legacy of those who worked and died constructing them. Certainly for some it was a "spiritual labour" but probably not for all…

Part of building signs of God's coming reign is to build institutions that display a character different from the spirit of our age. As Neil Postman has pointed out, institutions give meaning to our culture, and here we should add, institutions that reflect God's coming reign will do so even if they have to defy the logic of our age.[23] If one walks among the ancient stones of Columba's monastery on Iona one sees an institution that shadowed with meaningful love over the world of the ancient Picts in Scotland. The restoration and resurrection of those stones into Iona community by George McCleod and a small group of supporters is a powerful example of work as prayer on a journey that builds and rebuilds. This community, with members and associates spread throughout the world speaks of exactly the kind of institutional sign that carries forward the dynamic expression of work as prayer and prayer as work. This is expressed in the Iona Rule where members and associates pledge to contribute to the community in prayer, study, and communally shared means.[24]

This assertion for building institutions is in contrast to much of North American Church talk that remain stolidly anti-institutional. One example of this is Alan Hirsch's book, *The Forgotten Ways: Reactivating the Missional Church*.[25] Although Hirsch and others have much helpful to say about the dynamic nature of the Christian faith as a movement, they seem to assume that such movements do not institutionalise or that if they do it is necessarily the end of it. Their argument follows a business model that takes a consumer capitalist approach of competition among Christian communities as its basis.

Sociologically speaking almost all movements become institutions and such institutionalisation is not necessary harmful to its purpose. The history of the Christian faith is the history of movement and institution. All the great

Monastic orders followed such a path with much blessing. Not institutionalising may create many problems in terms of accountability and faithfulness to tradition. For one thing, institutions are able to create structures that advocate and work for justice where fragmented movements cannot effectively do so. When communities find standards and establish a Rule they are busy institutionalising what they have learned in a way to pass it along and to involve others in it. Such a process is an example of building signs for the reign of God. We can conclude then that the spirituality of the road will build institutions that sustain communities. Such communities are signs of God's coming reign.

Recently, in talking to the Director of Evangelism for a major denomination in the United States he mentioned that he had visited churches that had spontaneously developed in Vietnam. To his surprise he discovered that some of these churches started when they discovered a copy of the Book of Forms of the Church of Scotland. They quickly organised themselves and recognised one another by following this rule together. Of course, such an example causes a Presbyterian like myself who sometimes find myself frustrated by the book of rules to chuckle, but it also speaks of the power that a common rule can have to bring a movement together and to give it direction. Such rules require constant revision and measurement against the norm of Jesus the Messiah, but they do provide an element of vigorous spiritual work.

In the habit of **working hard on the way** in **eschatological living** we raise signs of God's coming reign. We also provide a foretaste.

We live in Such a Way of Love and Service that we Provide a Taste of What is to Come

> I come from a cultural tradition where making your own sausage is very important. There is of course a good recipe of ingredients and special spices. However, the way to ensure that it is made right we have the practice of tasting. After the mix is made little bits are fried up in pan and the family tastes and decides what spices need to be strengthened to make it just right. We can call these experiments foretastes.

For Christian spirituality to have substance as witness to Jesus the Messiah and as a sign of God's grace, we too will have to be constant experiments subjected to the ever-improved taste test. Do we give of the flavour, the aroma, the taste of the gracious reign of God in action and advocacy?

One of the earliest names given to followers of Jesus the Messiah was "The Way". This is an example of just how embodied the faith of the early Christians was. Of course, we do them and ourselves no service in romanticising their faith. However, they did understand that to be a Christian is to walk on the way of Jesus the Messiah ever improving on the way. With all the emphasis so far on being different from the present age and acting against the spirit of our age we may have the impression that the spirituality of the road is something deeply alien to those around us. Indeed, where the culture around us clambers for consumer self-satisfaction and boundless self-assertion the way of the Messiah may not be very welcome. However, there is another more profound truth. The way of the Messiah is the way that satisfies the deepest yearning of the human condition. If people cannot see this in the midst of our communities, if they do not get a foretaste of how this longing will be met by God, and if, in our relationships we cannot bring a taste of the age to come that makes others hunger for more, then there is something seriously wrong with our way. The way of the Messiah is not all negation; it lives out of the subtle but universe-transforming power of the resurrection. We provide a taste of the age to come as we walk in the kind of prayer that encounters God as Thou. This encounter allows us to find our true meaning and purpose. The metaphors of being salt and light in the world, used in the Gospels, speak of our taste giving function in the world. Even as we journey in a cruciform way we journey in joy, celebration, and hope.

North American Christian communities today rarely walk such a tasteful way. At best we demonstrate something that simply reflects our culture and its preferences, at worst we fight and slander one another worse than people in the culture around us! The *labora* of the spirituality of the road invites our journey in community to become qualitatively different in its love, in the way it brings together people of different cultures and races, in the way it focuses on those who are most on the margins, and in the way it lives to address the large systems of injustice in the global world. The work of such spirituality of taste is demonstrated in giving leadership in our society for justice and peace, both on a national and global scale and in the local community where we gather. Only when our way is walked like this will our hopes bring taste to our villages and cities.

There is also the temptation to expect utopia. History is fraught with failed attempts at creating utopian communities. Due to the imperfections with which we join the journey our foretaste as communities of faith is not in being unblemished examples, but rather in resilient travellers, that will pick up and continue on, believing and hoping again despite the failures of community. It is perhaps here where the great definition of love in 1 Cor. 13 becomes most challenging. Love does not keep a record of wrongs, it never gives up and its faith hope and patience never fail. In this very resilience of **eschatological living** lies the foretaste of God's coming reign.

We grow to Bear the Fruit of the Spirit of the Coming Messiah

In chapters 2 and 3 we have explored the many nuances of the fruit of the Spirit and its place in the journey of those formed for Christian leadership. These elements are captured in the habits of **covenant faithfulness, eschatological hope, loving self-giving sacrifice, transformation of the mind, worship, embodiment** and **human agency.** These habits also represent what is known in the New Testament as the fruit of the Spirit. These "fruit" in a direct way reflects the character and personality of Jesus the Messiah. When we live and reflect them, we are living in and reflecting the Holy Spirit. I would add that where such fruit is lived out by people who do not claim to be Christian they too bear witness to God's coming reign. Christianity as a religion or churches as institutions do not control or limit the profound presence of the Spirit of God in creation.

The embodied nature of being a sign, foretaste and first fruit of the coming reign of God makes us understand that these signs, and this foretaste and these fruits are sacramental in nature. In some way, in walking in this way, Christians on the road of spirituality embody and create signs of the grace of God. Our communities are signs, tastes, and fruit of God's approaching grace. Even our buildings on the street corner, our welcome to people who are from different cultures and walks of life, and our music broadcast for the world to hear, provide such sacramental presence. Most of all, our relationships with our neighbours, and our work-*labora* in love towards them, the marginalised and the healing of the cosmos serve as great sacramental and evangelical acts. Our resilience in the face of opposition, and love in the face of hatred, our hope in the face of despair, and faith in the face of cynicism all speak sacramentally and proclaim the Gospel of the Messiah who has come and is coming. We can thus claim that the spirituality of the road is a spirituality in sacramental community. Formation on this journey takes place in communion with a community.

No Spirituality without Community

The integration of all the theological reflection we have done so far is to be found in community. Community is a word with a many possible meanings. We therefore need to be clear what kind of community we speak of, and how one walks a road with such a community. To unpack this we need to return to the first Chapter of this book where we examined call. I argue here that the community we are called to have two loci. At the one end it includes the widest possible use of the English word community to embrace the whole of creation – the cosmos. On the other end the community with which we walk is a local band of followers of Jesus the Messiah with whom we walk in communion. It turns out that the 20th century feminist activist call, "think globally, act locally" captures that idea beautifully!

Let us start with the wide context of the community within which we journey. This community is the whole of creation. The problem with such a large concept is that it can be overwhelming and become so vague that it does not help us understand our place and our role in communion with it. We have to grasp creation theologically, by faith, in love seeking to understand and to find our role and journey within it. To do this we need to return to the story of creation. Faith begins with creation.

Spirituality is Communion with Creation

The story of creation has recently received much attention from theologians who try to develop an understanding of our responsibility towards the ecology of our biosphere. Some of the pioneers include Brian Swimme and Thomas Berry, and eco-feminist theologians such as Sally McFague. Theologians, particularly from an Asian context have also picked up this theme as they seek to include Asian tradition and philosophy with their Christian faith.[26] I find the work of Jürgen Moltmann particularly creative and respectful to the larger Christian tradition. Moltmann argues for a kind of panentheism. Panentheism, at least in the way Moltmann's ideas unfold, is the idea that God is beyond creation though also in some way present in it. In addition, Moltmann's vision also an en-pantheistic (creation existing in God) perspective. This is very different from what we can call stark monotheism – the idea that there is a complete and utter break between God and creation. The way the story of creation is told in Genesis suggests a God who is not just beyond creation but also is clearly deeply engaged with it. In addition Moltmann's theology argues for a correspondence between God as community and creation and humankind as community[27]. We have seen in an earlier chapter that Karl Barth related the idea of the image of God in Genesis 1 with the community of man and woman. This means that God is certainly beyond creation – "Thou" – and yet despite this Barthian emphasis we also have to conclude that God is also integrally connected with creation and sustains it particularly through the work of God's Spirit. We can see this correspondence in the shape of our argument so far in this book where our response to God as "Thou" is made possible by the Spirit of the Messiah at work within us.

Moltmann, following Isaac Luria (1554-1572) of Kabbalistic Judaism, argues for creation as something that is created *within* God.[28] I have emphasised this idea several times before in relation to Acts 17:28 which asserts that we live, move and exist in God. If God is all in all, then, the argument goes, for creation to come into being as other than God, God has to make space for it within God. God therefore voluntarily withdraws God-self to make space for the wonder and glory of creation. This act of Divine withdrawal is understood as an act of God's freedom to limit God-self. Of course, from a Christian point of view such an act of self-limitation in love is exactly what we understand the incarnation of Jesus the Messiah to be as well. It therefore appears that it is a divine characteristic that God in freedom makes room for others in love. God makes room for creation and thus stands as a "Thou" in relation to it, but, we learn from the Hebrews, that God is also constantly and intimately involved in the sustenance of creation. For one thing, the Spirit of God gives life. Therefore there is a sense in which God is beyond creation and relates to it, and there is also a sense in which creation itself as the work of God exists somehow in room or space made by God for it.

Of course, such philosophical reflection is absent in the pre-critical reflection of the original creation narratives that we find in Genesis. However, this logic as reflected in many stories in the Hebrew Scriptures that understand God as beyond creation yet actively involved in it and reflected in the Book of Acts, is quite convincing. Such logic allows us as post-enlightenment people to remythologise creation. It helps us to take the "universe story" that Brian Swimme and Thomas Berry developed and to understand it in the context of God whom we meet as "Thou" on the road of faith and who is also the one in whom all things live and move and exist. Such a vision makes it impossible to de-sacralise creation, it also makes it impossible to simply make creation into God. Yet, creation itself is sacramental in that it is a visible sign of God's grace.

Moltmann adds another twist to his reflection. He understands the creation process not just as something that has happened and is being sustained, he understands it, as an eschatological process. Creation is on its way to consummation. The new heaven and the new earth is to come. Moltmann thus argues that the Spirit does not only sustain creation and give life now, but that the Spirit also journeys with creation in transformative action for final consummation. This he describes as the three creation tasks undertaken by the Spirit of God, *creatio continua* (the continuing life giving sustenance), *creatio nova* (the process of making creation new), *creatio anticipative* (the process of anticipating the coming new creation).[29] He concludes,

> The creation of liberty, righteousness and salvation in human history initiates the fulfilment of that promise which creation as the beginning represent in its very self.[30]

This vision of Moltmann, grounded in the Scriptural text and focused on God's work in creation in the Holy Spirit is not without its critics.[31] However, what Moltmann achieves is to provide us with a vision of God's work through creation both in its original form and in its eschatological journey. It is also a vision that makes particular sense of the unfolding of the Biblical story of creation and redemption. It clearly focuses on God's work and the eschatological journey of creation as a community of God. It also offers room for us to understand our own place within that eschatological journey of God with creation and us. Most importantly, when we move beyond the abstraction of this vision of the unfolding creation, we can imagine how ongoing creation sustains us, how the coming new creation is already with us, and how the coming new creation – the anticipatory creation – draws us forward as we walk on a spiritual journey.

Moltmann helpfully frames the work of the Spirit in terms of the drive towards liberty, righteousness and salvation. How does a spirituality of the road live out this threefold work of the Spirit? To unpack this we will explore the fruitfulness of Moltmann's vision in terms of the concepts of **meaning, identity, fracture, direction**, and **task**. It will be made clear that these five themes also coincide with the habits of Christian spirituality we have unpacked earlier.

First, to understand the creation of which we are a part as something so cherished by God that God made space for it in Divine withdrawal is to give profound **meaning** to creation and to our own existence in it. The constant and repeated cherishment of creation in the Genesis 1 creation account – and God saw that it was good – speaks of the meaning of all things that exist. The spirituality of the road lives out of and moves in communion with the reality of the meaningfulness of everything in creation. As such, this link between the meaning of embodied things, and God's sustaining love for it is to be part of both the work and prayer of a follower of Christian spirituality in community. It is therefore impossible to conceive of a person on the path of Christian spirituality **not** paying attention to the care of the environment, the beauty of tending and caring for gardens, animals and the ecosphere. Ignoring the human destruction of creation is a profound act of sin and rebellion. This sin is echoed in Paul's words, "For we know that up to the present time all of creation groans with pain, like the pain of childbirth." (Rom 8:22 GNB). To walk in communion with creation is to cherish and care for it where we are and to advocate for its care throughout the planet.

Second, to understand creation as something so valuable to God, that God would seek to have communion with it, helps us understand how vital this communion with creation is for our spiritual journeys. In Genesis 2:3 we find God blessing the seventh day and therefore blessing time. The Genesis 1 account of creation describes the days (time) as the structure of the created order. This blessing of time, corresponding to God's enjoyment of creation in the refrain "and God saw that it was good" in Genesis 1 relays the importance of the whole of creation not just humankind. This divine cherishment of creation suggests that our **identity** as humans is tied in with creation itself. First we are part of creation and secondly we are those who are given the task to care for it with and in the Spirit. The arrogance of the Western Industrial Revolution and the reductionist scientific mindset that makes creation into an exploitable commodity and object is a profound sin. If we find our identity as creatures, we will not brook the exploitation and destruction of creation.

Unfortunately Christian communities have generally speaking not been in the forefront of opposing the relentless march of technological exploitation of the planet. We do not seem ready to change our sinful ways. Those on the path of Christian spirituality operating out of its identity in creation will have to challenge and lead people into a profound repentance away from creation-exploiting behaviour aimed at our self-satisfaction. To walk in communion with creation is to walk in a new way with it and for it.

Third, the renewing work of the Spirit and the eschatological direction of its healing and transformative work in creation chalenges us to understand the importance of the **fracture** of creation as a result of human hubris. In the Western Christian tradition we have called this "The Fall" and it is symbolised of human self-reliance in the Garden of Eden. Being East of Eden means that we are broken and that we are in a process of breaking God's creatures and creation. Such belief is unpopular today. Recently a minister who leads a congregation who has moved to "contemporary worship" told me that he has dispensed with the traditional approach of God in worship with confession of sin and prayers of repentance. He deemed such ideas old-fashioned and out of step with our present culture. Yet, we live, at least in North America, in a culture so far East of Eden that we resist any form of caring for creation that costs us something. We live in a global culture where genocides continue to happen and where our governments seem only to fund and support international interventions if there is something in it for them. We are broken, and we continue to fracture relationships, people, and creation. The spirituality of the road confronts our profound brokenness with constant repentance and calls for those who walk with us to turn for the reign of God is near. To walk in communion with creation is to live out of such ongoing spirit of repentance.

Fourth, our **direction** is towards the transforming work of the Spirit that we have thus far described as living eschatologically from the power of the coming reign of God. The spirituality of the road lives exactly out of the work of the Spirit of Jesus the Messiah that is the new creation (*creatio nova*) plus the anticipated coming creation (*creatio anticipative*). This means we live out of the resurrection as summons. Our brokenness, our failure, our weakness, is made whole in the work of the Spirit. This work, as we have seen above which is sign, foretaste, and first fruit, finds its inspiration (literally its in-breathing by the Spirit) in the link of the work of the transformation of the whole of creation.[32] The spirituality of the road lives in the direction towards such transformation in communion with creation. The leadership that emerges from this kind of spirituality will draw on the habit of **eschatological living.**

Finally, the four dimensions described above, meaning, identity, fracture, and direction all imply a **task.** The spirituality of the road in communion with creation is an *activist* spirituality. It is, to use our traditional Benedictine language: *labora.* Such labour occurs in work and prayer as the liturgy below implies,

> Mwari Father, I have come today to plant your trees. I have come with the *mutumbu* tree to pay for my transgression [of earth destruction]. I place them here in your soil. You tree, I place you in this soil. Grow! Become tall, wax strong! Even if the hail from the heavens hits you, I want you to remain alive... through the coming ages. My friend whom I love, I shall come to visit often to see you. Stay right here where I plant you. (Bishop Marinada, 1993)[33]

This prayer liturgy by Bishop Marinda of an Africa Initiated Church in Zimbabwe demonstrates how the spirituality of the road brings together our place in creation and our task with and for it. Zimbabwe has been catastrophically deforested over the last 40 years. Efforts made by Inus (M.L.) Daneel to bring environmental awareness to the fast growing Africa Initiated Churches brought a sea change in attitude that fed into massive tree planting services complete with a prayer liturgy like the one above. The prayer includes both the recognition of fracture and repentance from it as well as earth healing transformative action. The spirituality that feeds this action is deeply rooted in theology.

Bishop Marinda demonstrates Christian leadership for the healing and transformation of creation in an exemplary way. It reminds us of the famous story, which according to my knowledge, has never been verified, that Martin Luther said that if he knew the world was going to go the pieces he would go plant an apple tree.[34]

Building for and with the reign of God means working for the care and renewal of creation while anticipating the coming new creation. It means the affirmation of matter. It means the cherishment of body. It means the care for and protection of animal and plant life. It means planting and creating. It means that life is sacred – of the Spirit. Christian spirituality in this way requires wise action for the good of creation, and leading Christian communities into understanding this as part of their Gospel obedience. This is how wide we need to understand walking in community with creation.

Thus far then our discussion of the journey in communion with creation. However, the spirituality of the road acts locally in community with the local Christian community as well. What does this mean, how is it rooted in our theological understanding and what shape does this take? How do we lead for and in community and why should we?

Spirituality in Communion with the Local Christian Community

We need to commence once again with theology if we want to understand the pivotal importance of the local embodied community in the spirituality of the road. In my view one of the great gains made in theological reflection during the last half of the twentieth century has been the link made between a Trinitarian understanding of God and the Christian community. One of the chief proponents of this way of thinking has been Jürgen Moltmann, but his student Miroslav Volf has convincingly built this link into a full fledged understanding of the church in his book *After our Likeness: The Church as the Image of the Trinity*.[35] Volf also complains that references to the Trinity and community have become so commonplace in theological reflection that it is in danger of losing its specific meaning.[36] Of course, his book aims to correct that! The thinking is basically this: We learn from the doctrine of the Trinity that God is a community of Trinitarian persons that are also one in mutual love and self-giving. This conception of God is called the Social Trinity. The concept of self-giving is expressed in the ancient doctrine of *perichoresis*. *Perichoresis* is the Greek word used for the idea of the constant process of self-giving among persons of the Trinity that goes back to Gregory of Nazianzus (329-389?) and John of Damascus (676-749). It is beyond the scope of this discussion to develop a theology of the church (ecclesiology) based in the social Trinity, I have attempted this elsewhere.[37] What is important here is to link this concept of the Social Trinity to the idea of a spirituality of the road in community. Let us explore the logic of the link between God as a community, and the church and our local communities:

Through Jesus the Messiah, and Jesus' unique relationship with the Father and the Spirit we have a window into the very heart of the Godhead. This does not mean that we are as arrogant as to claim that we know anything definitive about God's inner life, rather we humbly draw on God's actions in the world as we understand it to give us a window into a limited but profound insight about God. Through this window as displayed in the life, ministry, death and resurrection of Jesus, we see that the relationship among Father, Son and Spirit is one of complete self-giving love to one another. This argument assumes with Jürgen Moltmann and Karl Rahner that God as revealed in God movement to us in Jesus the Messiah shows us something essential about what God is like in God-self. This idea is somewhat humorously captured in what is often called "Rahner's Rule" the immanent Trinity (what God is like in God-self) is equal to the economic Trinity (what God is shown to be in God's saving and judging actions towards the world). Perhaps equal is too broad a term, I would rather assert that we knowing something limited but true about God in God-self.

For the sake of our exploration of the spirituality of the road it is important to see that this revelation of the likeness of God as community in perfect loving communion is also a dispostion we are called to reflect on our journeys. In Chapter 1 we followed Breuggemann, Sailhammer and Barth's argument that the creation of humankind as male and female in the first creation account points to the essential communal nature of God reflected in the human community. We have also noted Jürgen Moltmann's argument for an analogy of relationship (*analogia relationis*) between humans created in God's image and God. The fracture of creation is also demonstrated in the breaking of community in Genesis 3. This means that the redemption of creation is fundamentally connected to the restoration of community and life-giving relationship among humans and creation. But this is not just a vague sense of "community" it is a very specific God-reflecting, God-imaging kind of community. It is to be a sign in the world of what God is like. It is a community in diversity that gives self to the other in constant love. In the theological language of Saint John of Damascus we describe this as a *perichoretic* community. It makes sense then, when God covenants with Abraham that God does not just covenant for the sake of Abraham, but God covenants for the sake of the restoration of blessing – communion with God – for all peoples. We have also seen how N.T. Wright has described this task of the blessing of all nations – the bringing together of diversity in community – as the core of God's redemptive promise for creation. Moreover, Wright shows convincingly that this plan is also the core of what Paul understands as the Gospel of salvation.

If we follow this argument through to the local Christian community things fall into place. The task of bringing the Gospel of reconciliation to the nations is the task of the local community on a journey. The task of Christian spirituality is to walk with the community into such a process of bringing together of people who are different in reconciled loving self-giving community in communion with God (prayer, praise, and worship). This task is accomplished by loving our neighbours, being companions to the marginalised, or if marginalised, accepting companionship in resistance, and bringing healing to the cosmos. The task is empowered and transformed in the midst of the doxological worship of God in community. The spirituality of the road in communion with the local Christian community is nothing less than walking on this road in example, leadership and service. A community that walks together on this road becomes a sign, a foretaste, and a first-fruit and thus a *sacrament* of the coming redemptive reign of God.

Another word, which is inherently biblical, that can be used for the character of the local community that we join in lead is *hospitality*. The spirituality of the road is a hospitable process. Hospitality, sharing food and shelter and providing sanctuary, gives expression to such a community and such spirituality. As I acknowledged elsewhere, hospitality is not without its own problems. It may appear a one-way process as Letty Russell points out.[38] However, in its biblical form it takes on the form of *mutual* self-giving. We can say that the idea of divine self-giving (*perichoresis*) is essentially an idea of divine hospitality. The incarnation of God in Jesus teaches us that this is not an invitation to the guest to become like the host or to become beholden unto the host, but an invitation to the guest to become themselves in relationship to the host. It is in this light that we read Paul's words,

> So there is no difference between Jews and Gentiles, between slaves
> and free people, between men and women; you are all one in union
> with Christ Jesus. (Gal. 3:28, GNB)

Such hospitality and such community in self-giving cannot be disembodied, it cannot be "spiritualised" to vague attitudes it requires a concrete people in a place – a local Christian community. As Bryan Stone puts it,

> To offer Christ to the world is to offer the world a people, a body
> that may truly be spoken of as "Christ's," created and formed by the
> Holy Spirit as that space.[39]

The spirituality of the road walks a road of being formed into such a community
and such a body. There is no Christian spirituality and even no road to walk in
without community.

To Conclude: The Spirituality of the Road as Martyria – Witness

All that has gone before speak of the essential witness character of a spirituality
embodied in communion and community. In 2007 I had the pleasure to receive
Sam Wells, at the time Dean of Duke University Chapel, in a theological class
to speak to my students about Ecclesial Ethics. In response to a student who
wanted him to make ecclesial ethics concrete he asked what would have happened if, the day after September 11, George Bush appeared on television and
said something like this, "This has been a horrific and painful act of aggression.
Our hearts go out to those who lost loved ones in the United States and all over
the world. It is an act with dark and evil intent. It is an act of violence. Yet, we
are a Christian nation; therefore we are enjoined to love our enemy and to forgive. We are constrained by our faith not to respond to violence with violence.
Therefore, what we need to do in response is to heal our broken hearts and then
to bring justice through peaceful means and seek reconciliation with those who
have done such an evil act." He suggested that what would have happened in
such a case is true Christian witness to the Gospel of Jesus the Messiah. The
spirituality of the road is always unapologetically political and uncomfortably
radical in this way.

The embodiment of the Gospel is not an easy affair. The spirituality of
the road is costly. Sometimes even costly to the point of letting go of our own
salvation… When asked by one of those who plotted to kill Hitler during the
Second World War, if God would ever forgive them for such an act, Dietrich
Bonhoeffer is reported to have responded, "I don't know if God can ever forgive
us, but I do know that we have no choice but to go ahead." The juxtaposition
of these two stories shows just how complex it can be to walk the way in one's
present circumstances. One perspective saw non-violence as the only way; the
other saw limited violence for the greater good, even though it may mean the
loss of one's own communion with God. My argument here is not that what
we have explored so far makes anything simple or easy. It is hugely complicat-
ed to walk the way of witness as leaders in Christian communities today. It has
always been. There are therefore no neat prescriptions. There is, however, a

journey to make together, a road to walk and debates to have. Formation for Christian spirituality proceeds from the assumption that this road less travelled, the sacramental road, is the way to go. It is bearing costly witness on the way – *martyria*. John Howard Yoder makes clear how this costly witness operates,

> The believer's cross must be, like his Lord's the price of his social non-conformity. It is not, like sickness or catastrophe, an inexplicable, unpredictable suffering; it is the end of a path freely chosen after counting the cost... it is the social reality of representing in an unwilling world the Order to come.[40]

Of course the path (road) freely chosen while counting the cost is taken in obedience as we have seen earlier. The free choice is made, even as we recognise that it is the Spirit of the Messiah at work within us. We may be tempted to make witness into something that is only heroic. We could point to some of those great witnesses of our time and history such as Rosina Mpashlele, Mother Teresa, Dietrich Bonhoeffer, Archbishop Romero, Desmond Tutu, and others. The truth is that usually witness calls us to a dull and ordinary resilience in the face of the many small choices and many debilitating but ordinary disappointments we face every day.

We may be tempted to seek the great heroic task while missing the heroism of the dusty and unglamorous road of our local community. It is to persist in witness when no one is watching and when no news reporters will come. To take small actions of compassion and make small sacrifices for the sake of the community without telling. To have hope when the pundits tell us that people are leaving the church in droves. To persist in love when the local community of faith appears as fractured and fractious and behaving in ways worse than the world around it. To serve a small rural community that is in no danger of becoming a mega-church. To love the unlovely when even our community cannot find it in their hearts. To work at helping people of different cultures and traditions to worship together in difference and love. These are the marks of *martyria*. It is tough, but it is easy in the love and embrace of the Spirit of the Messiah. Only if we are called into being and called on the road by the creative Word of God will we be able to do so.

In the final analysis walking this way is a sacrament of the coming reign of God and true evangelism. Bryan Stone writes,

> If the primary logic of evangelism is *witness* rather than achievement, accomplishment, or production, then it is the character of the per-

formance rather than the implementation of an assumed end that defines excellent practice.[41]

This reminds us that the final step in our exploration of Christian spirituality is to turn to **mission**.

Notes

1. Breuggemann, W. *Genesis: Interpretation - A Bible Commentary for Teaching and Preaching.* Atlanta: John Knox Press, 1982, 145.

2. Breuggemann, W. *The Creative Word: Canon as a Model for Biblical Education.* Philadelphia: Fortress Press, 1982. Breuggemann actually argues that he deals with Biblical Education, but his insights are just as applicable to formation for Christian leadership in general.

3. Cited in Breugemann, Ibid., 102.

4. Ibid., 94-95.

5. Thus the Rule of Saint Benedict include instructions on how many Psalms should be said in the night office (Chapter 9), in what order the Psalms are to be said (Chapter 18) and the manner of reciting the Psalms (Chapter 19). The rule also includes and instructions on learning the Psalms and many chapters give more detailed instructions on how many Psalms have to be said.

6. Breuggemann, Ibid., 101.

7. Benedict, *The Holy Rule of Saint Benedict* (Translated by B. Verheyen) (http://www.ccel.org/ccel/benedict/rule.html) 3.

8. The concept of the "prevenient grace of God" is interpreted differently in different Christian traditions, but all of them agree that God's grace is the basis and basic cause of human action.

9. Breuggemann, Ibid., 102-103.

10. "We shall have profited admirably in the sacrament, if the thought shall have been impressed and engraven on our minds, that none of our brethren is hurt, despised, rejected, injured, or in any way offended, without our, at the same time, hurting, despising, and injuring Christ; …" Calvin, J. *The Institutes of the Christian Religion. Book IV. Chapter 17:38*translated by H. Beverage. Grand Rapids: Eerdmans, 1957, 2596.

11. Fensham, C.J. *Emerging from the Dark Age Ahead: The Future of the North American Church.* Toronto: Clements Academic. 2011.

12. Sölle, D. *Thinking About God.* London: SCM, 1990, p.5.

13. Wright, Ibid., 245.

14. Cited in Goheen, M *"As the Father Has Sent Me, I Am Sending You":J. E. Lesslie Newbigin's Missionary Ecclesiology"* 46.

15. Ukpong, J. "Essay in Inculturation Biblical Hermeneutic." *Semeia* (73, 2000) 189-210.

16. McCarroll, P. *Waiting for the Thief in the Night: The Character of Christian Hope in the Theology of the Cross for the North American Context.* Toronto: Toronto School of Theology, Unpublished Ph.D. thesis, 2006. 17.

17. John 1:46 "Can anything good come from Nazareth?" Nathanael asked. "Come and see," answered Philip.

18. Dawn, M.J *Reaching Out Without Dumbing Down: A Theology of Worship for This Urgent Time.* Grand Rapids: Eerdmans, 1995, 108. (the repeated lines indicated in the Dawn text have been added here).

19. Moltmann, J. *Experiences in Theology.* Minneapolis: Fortress Press, 2000. p. 43

20. Bosch, D.J. *Transforming Mission: Paradigm Shifts in Theology of Mission* New York: Orbis Books, 1991, 233. Bosch cites Newman, J.H. *Historical Sketches Volume II.* Westminster: Christian Classics Inc. 1830, 411.

21. Newbigin, L. *The Household of God: Lectures on the Nature of the Church.* London: SCM, 1953.

22. Kearney, R.*The God who May Be.* Bloomington: Indianna University Press, 2001. 52.

23. Postman, N. *Technopoly: The Surrender of Culture to Technology.* New York: Alfred A. Knopf. 1992. 74.

24. See http://www.iona.org.uk/iona_rule.php (accessed August 26, 2009)

25. Hirsch, A. *The Forgotten Ways: Reactivating the Missional Church* Grand Rapids: Baker Books, 2006.

26. Providing a bibliography for eco-theology is beyond the scope of this book, however, three excellent examples of an Asian engagement with eco-theology are, Lee, Jai-Don. "Towards an Asian Ecotheology in the Context of Thomas Berry's Cosmology." Ph.D. diss., University of St. Michael's College, 2004. and Lee, Jeong Guk, *Celebrating God's Cosmic Perichoresis: The Eschatological Panentheism of Jürgen Moltmann as a Resource for an Ecological Christian Worship* Eugene Oregon: Pickwick Publications, 2011, and Choi, Moon-jung, A Critical Examination of the Implications of Sallie McFague's Theological Method for a Korean. Th.M. thesis, Knox College, University of Toronto, 2009.

27. Moltmann argues for an analogy of relationship (*analogia relationis*) between God and humankind based in the idea that the image of God is carried by humankind in its relationality. See, Moltmann, J. *God in Creation.* New York: Harper Row, 1985, 77ff.

28. Moltmann, J. *God in Creation.* San Francisco: Harper Row, 1985, 87.

29. Ibid., 209.

30. Ibid.

31. See Jeong Guk Lee's discussion of this in his footnote, Lee, J.G. Ibid., footnote 189.

32. One of the challenges of contemporary eco-theology is its tendency to absolutise creation as it is, so, this critique is expressed in Harold Wells' complaint that Sally McFague's concept of creation as "body of God" reifies creation to the point that one cannot transform and change things. He argues that such a proposal contain a conservatism, a deradicalisation and domestication of the doctrine of creation that does not allow for the importance of the transformative and healing task we are to engage. I do think, in response to Wells' critique, that McFague tries to address this by means of advancing agential plus process metaphors of God's ongoing engagement in creation. See Wells, H. *The Christic Center: Life-Giving and Liberating* New York: Orbis Books, 2004, 128-130 and see McFague. Sally *The Body of God: An Ecological Theology.* Minneapolis: Fortress Press. 139-141.

33. Daneel, M.L. *African Earthkeepers:Wholistic Interfaith Mission.* New York: Orbis Books, 2001, 185.

34. McKim. D. (Ed.) *The Cambridge Companion to Martin Luther.* Cambridge: Cambridge University Press, 2003, 162.

35. Volf, M. *After Our Likeness: The Church as the Image of the Trinity.* Grand Rapids: Eerdmans, 1998).

36. Ibid., 191.

37. See Fensham, Ibid. 2008.

38. Russell, L.M. *The Church in the Round: Feminist Interpretation of the Church.* Westminster: John Knox, 1993, 173. See my discussion in Fensham, C.J. *Emerging from the Dark Age Ahead: The Future of the North American Church.* Toronto: Clements Academic, 2011, 75-76.

39. Stone, Ibid., 110.

40. Cited in Stone, Ibid., 279.

41. Ibid., 277.

5

Send

*Who would true valour see let them come
hither:
Here's one will constant be
Come wind, come weather.
There's no discouragement shall make me
once relent
My first avowed intent to be a pilgrim*
                                   —(JOHN BUNYAN, 1628-1688)

The diesel engine throbbed in deep base tones under our feet as the great Pacific Ocean slid under our feet. There were no cabins on this small freighter, nor a lounge for travellers. Our sleeping bags were rolled out under the stars come wind, come weather. It did come in the form of a strong soaking downpour that cooled the tropic humidity and within and hour we were dry again. About us were another twenty people taking a slow boat to the outer islands of the French Polynesian archipelago. Our destination was Rangiroa, the big atoll circle in the ocean. We were sent by the local church as a group of three pilgrims to dramatise Gospel stories in regional worshipping communities. Accompanying Alain, a local teen with a penchant for acting, we traveled to dramatise Gospel stories in local communities. It was to be a two week trip. Upon arrival at the small pier on Rangiroa we were greeted by a band of children frolicking in the water and the local pastor. "How are you getting back?" was his first, somewhat anxious question, after the greetings were out of the way. "We are taking this boat in two weeks, when it calls here again", I said. "Oh", said the pastor, "as far as I know it will only be back in three months..." By that time the little freighter had already unloaded and had pulled out into the ocean on its rounds to another small community. There was no way of knowing when we would get back…

The little freighter showed up two weeks later in the middle of the worship service that involved every hand on the island. Worship was abruptly stopped and after tearful goodbyes, and within fifteen minutes, we were installed on the deck drifting back to Papeete, Tahiti.

There are no guarantees for home comfort on the way of the pilgrim, sent to the ends of the earth to witness for the Gospel! Wind and weather will come. Opposition, derision or indifference will appear. Even persecution may occur. Yet the way of the Christian faith from that earliest moment of commissioning to today remains the way of those sent into the world. Most journeys will not be as remote a sojourn as Rangiroa, nor as placid, yet, whether we are sent far away or sent to the neighbourhood close to home, one fact remains without question, every Christian is being sent. "Sentness" is the basic stance of the Christian life. It is the culmination of worship and praise as we move from being called to community, to listening, to journeying, to receiving God's sacraments to being sent. We are sent to be sacramental in the world. Such a state of being sent is always in the disposition of the pilgrim. On this journey we are to hold our securities lightly. Our home comforts are a blessing to be enjoyed and embraced but not to be taken for granted on the way.

"Call", our first theme of this book, already implies a sending. The creative Word of God calls us into being. We are called into being a community as humans together symbolised in the creation of man and woman thus being images of the nature of God as communion in love. We have argued that this God-imaging community is not defined by the biological difference between male and female but rather by the human capacity for community creating love. We are called and sent on our own *peregrinatio pro Christi* in community to the neighbour, the marginalised, the diversity of nations, and the cosmos. We are justified and sent in the Spirit of the Messiah. Our task is living in covenant faithfulness, eschatological hope, self-giving sacrifice, transformation of the mind, worship, embodied living in creation, and the work of our effort. In Jesus the Messiah, and through our neighbour's need we discover who we are. It is for this high calling that we are formed in Christian spirituality. We are called to be signs, a foretaste, and fruit – a sacrament – of the God's reign that is coming. We are called to be witnesses and in this way to be pilgrims on a journey. We are called to lead others on the pilgrim journey – the journey of the spirituality of the road.

Formation for Christian spirituality in community is an apostolic task. The word apostolic is derived from the Greek word "to send". We are to reflect the apostolic nature – the nature in mission – of the church as expressed in the ancient Creed when it says that the Church is one, holy, catholic and apostolic[1]. It is a task in which we invest our effort while always praying and recognising that all effort and strength comes from God's Spirit at work within us. With John Bunyan we need the Spirit that will enable our hearts to say,

> "There is no discouragement shall make me once relent my avowed intent to be a pilgrim. Hobgoblin nor foul fiend can daunt my spirit. I know I at the end shall life inherit. Then, fancies, flee away! Fear not what others say; I'll labour night and day to be a pilgrim."

This indomitable spirit of resilience and perseverance – the monastic spirit – is the spirit for which we are formed on the journey of formation. The task is thus a missional task. The journey is a journey in mission.

In this chapter we shall strive to integrate the reflections of call, listening, journey, sacrament and sending in a theology of formation for Christian spirituality. Throughout the preceding chapters I have emphasised the dynamic journeying "on the way" character of this approach to Christian spirituality. The word "mission" or the creedal concept "apostolic" are two ways that the church has often spoken of this dynamic reality. Spirituality in the missional sense is a verb. In addition, this dynamic process of forming missional spirituality also reflects the basic conviction that formation for Christian spirituality is an act of worship and follows the ancient logic of the worship of God. The context of worship places us in our rightful place in relation to God. God is God and the world is God's creation. Moreover, worship is an activity of community in communion with God's creation. We can therefore not speak of mission or the sending out of God's people without in the same breath speaking of the community of God's people – the church that is always emerging in the world in new ways as a sacramental sign of God's promise.

At this point the theological building blocks are in place, the plans are drawn; now we move towards the plan of action. Even so, as I have hoped to argue thus far, such plans are plans of spirit, disposition, virtue if you wish, rather than plans of technique and manipulation. Our great challenge, particularly in our technologically stamped present world, is not to reduce Christian spirituality in mission to a set of techniques. Rather than technique a better way of thinking of formation for Christian spirituality is to think of it in terms of relationship. Relationships are dynamic and organic. Relationships grow and pass through ebb and flow. Relationships are journeys that bring together the constant challenge of change, experience, emotion and thought. Relationships require communication. All these characteristics are also true of spirituality. Christian spirituality is rooted in relationship in community. When we are being sent into God's creation in mission we are therefore being sent in, with, and from community. This community includes communion with God in worship and communion with one another in relationship.

> *We can therefore not speak of Christian spirituality in the church emerging in mission without speaking of community.*

What is the architecture of communities of formation for Christian spirituality? How do we proceed to participate in this process called into action by God's creative Word and enthused by the Spirit of the Messiah?

Formation for Christian spirituality in mission grows in two particular contexts. The first is the local Christian community. The second is the journey towards the other (creation and neighbour). The Christian community remains the primary context of formation and the one that holds first responsibility. Traditionally, Christians have spoken about the nurturing or forming of people for spirituality in terms of being a *seminary*. This word basically means seed-bed. We are thus seedlings being nurtured in community for the task of spirituality. The local community is the *seminary* that is there to shape us and nurture us. However, this seed metaphor is not exhaustive. Mission implies sending, going on the road and walking the way. We have to add that we need to be on the journey to be properly formed. In fact, we cannot progress in Christian spirituality without engaging the dusty road towards others. This second context, the context of engagement is therefore equally important for our formation. This journey unfolds in the creation of beauty; the service of others; working for justice and peace; worship; the management of resources; the encouragement of our fellow travellers; the teaching of the Christian traditions; the shaping of new generations, and above all prayer.

The Local Christian Community as Seminary.

It is when the local community understands itself as called on a journey to the neighbour, the nations, marginalised, and the cosmos and lives out of this pilgrim existence that it can truly be a seed-bed of apostolic formation. The shape of the community itself and its missional direction is the first imprint on the person being formed. When children and youth see teens and young adults as well as grown members of the community work at these tasks they are inspired and invited on the journey of formation. To use contemporary ways of speaking, our communities construct us on the journey.

> I have recently experienced this with a teen that went to train for leadership in a Christian camping environment. He claimed that he loved the camp and the kids but that he was an atheist because all this "god-stuff" did not make sense in the "scientific" world he lived in. He particularly found the Bible hard to understand with many things that seemed wrong to him like celebrating the bashing of babies' heads against stones! Upon his return he told me that he can now think of himself as a Christian. I asked him what had changed for him during his training. He pointed to two pivotal moments. One was when the Director of a major Christian relief agency came to talk to them about the missional task of the church in caring for those in need around the world. He shared stories of Christian believers who make an impact on the world around them in their own commitment and journey. This was a revelation to this teen. He had the impression from some of the local Christian communities he was exposed to that they were only about getting together with the friends and having a good time at church events. The second pivotal moment was a young adult instructor who shared his own journey of faith with them. This included a sharing of his struggles and questions and the comfort and faith that was evoked in him through reading 1 John 4:7 ff., "Beloved, let us love one another; for love is of God, and he who loves is born of God and knows God…"

This young man encountered some of the key dimensions of formation in community. Besides the disciplines of prayer, bible study and worship that his program required, there was a focus on God's call to mission. The formational context demonstrated how to concretely live in the contemporary world with others on the journey. This context included caring for campers, seeking the best for them, protecting them, teaching them, and sharing both their struggles and discoveries of faith. The context challenged him to work with kids with disabilities and to seek to make them fully at home in the community. Through this community in mission and through his neighbours in the form of the kids he was responsible for, some with difficult problems, he started to encounter the missional Spirit of the Messiah.

Local Christian communities seldom understand their task as identifying, encouraging, forming and sending people on such a pilgrim journey. At best such action seems to be delegated to the ordained leader or a few special people in the community. This is the deep poverty in our local communities. When I examine locally constructed "mission statements" of Christian communities I have yet to find one that states, "We are pilgrims on a journey with the task to call, encourage and shape others..." This despite that ringing command in Matthew 28:20 "Teach them to obey everything I have commanded you..." Like the culture around us we are often too focused on ourselves, too pre-occupied with paying the bills and too poor a reflection of God's pilgrim people. Yet our task for which we are called into being is to be as sign, foretaste, and first fruit of God's coming reign. Within this task lies the obligation to engage God's mission in our task of formation. The church that emerges in mission is a people-forming church.

What then are the characteristics of a local Christian community that forms people in Christian spirituality? Given our discussion so far, the characteristics can be outlined in terms of faithfulness to call, listening, journey, sacrament, and sending. The community as a whole will take on this shape. In most Christian communities these elements already make up the structure of their worship. To make this shape clear people in the community have to understand its meaning. We should grasp this shape and this task as part of our identity – our apostolic task, our mission. We can call this the mission-shaped local Christian community.

To make this happen such a community will live out of the Scriptural Narrative of God's promise for the cosmos. This seems a point almost too basic to make, yet it is critical. *The whole community needs to understand its identity within the greater narrative of God's creating and loving purpose.* Each person needs to see their place as called to be in community and called to tend for God's people and creation. To do this such local Christian communities will tell and retell this story as part of the formation of its identity, and will help all its members from early age to understand the profound meaning of their existence as creatures. In a basic way this is about making connections. Often, people have a lot of knowledge about Christian faith and the Bible acquired over years, yet the wisdom of connecting this together in one great story of the meaning of our existence and how this leads to being sent into the world is lacking. We are not talking here about academic knowledge only, or philosophy, we are talking about the wisdom of living life meaningfully.

Every year I ask the students in my College in their second year to write me the story of God's intent for creation in one paragraph. It is sobering to discover how hard it is for students, who presumably have been formed to some extent on their Christian journey, to do so. At that point many are not yet immersed in the story and have a very vague perception of what they are called to be and where they are called to go. Their Christian journey is one constructed from multiple experiences and incidental insights rather than from a comprehensive grasp of the meaning of creation. Their insights mirror an internet search with several hits but little integrative wisdom. Knowledge is available in brilliant bursts, but is present as information, rather than as an integrated meaningful wisdom.   Immersing – baptising – people in this story as meaningful wisdom for life is the primary responsibility of the local Christian community as seed-bed for mission.

Facing Discouragement on the Way

There is no such thing as a perfect community; there will be disappointments, difficult people to deal with, major discouragements, and hurts for the learner along the journey. Being a Christian community as sign in the world is very much like the building of monasteries in the medieval period, it takes strength and tenacity to keep building and encouraging through the fickle realities of petty disagreements and hurtful relationships and disasters that will arise. Sometimes, even violent destruction of the community may occur. Yet, when we understand our true identity we shall work, we shall build, and we shall persevere even if only two of three are gathered. It is inevitable that things will always be imperfect because of our broken state. Perhaps Paul's realisation of the difficulty of the task as expressed in Romans 8:23 says it all, "But it is not just creation alone which groans; we who have the Spirit as the first of God's gifts also groan within ourselves as we wait for God to make us his children and set our whole being free." In this passage we are assured that God's Spirit sighs and groans for us and with us in the difficulty of the task and thus we are inspired to continue in the face of and despite all opposition and failure. Ours is not a mission based in quick fixes and quarterly results, ours is a mission within the time-span of creation itself. We may never taste the results on our own journey. It is with this assurance and in the indomitable power of the Holy Spirit that we are working out our salvation in fear and trembling.

As with the teen mentioned above, exposure to others committed to walk the path and seeing the examples of their faith is crucial. Resilience to follow the way is nurtured by such examples and particularly by mentorship on such a way. One of the most enlightening social studies done in the 20th century was the longitudinal study of Hawaiian children at risk. This study found that a major predictor for a well-adjusted adult person and parent was finding a mentor outside one's family who provided encouragement and a positive and alternative role model to the dismal conditions during childhood.[2] Of course, this study simply confirms what we know on many other levels in life and what is practiced by such organisations as Big Sisters and Big Brothers. As Christian communities we have to grasp the pivotal role of inter-generational mentorship for youth and children in our midst. Christian discipleship already implies mentorship as a basic condition of the Christian community, in addition we have examples of mentoring models in the Scriptural text such as Paul and Timothy and the tender care with which Timothy was mentored by the apostle. To be a seed-bed-seminary our local communities will have to understand themselves as mentoring institutions. Such mentoring cannot be left to chance, it has to be prayerfully planned and engaged with respect and care. In the process it will provide for the instructions of faith content and for inviting learners to engage the habits of *ora* et *labora*. In prayer and in work such local communities are always in a never-ending process of discernment to find those called to lead.

Formation includes the great virtues or habits that we have outlined in this book, but these are fed through the learning of content – the learning of the tradition. The study of the Scriptures, and particularly its *responsible* study, is pivotal. The teen referred to above could not find meaning in the Scriptures because he was exposed to a naïve and simplistic reading of the Bible. Unfortunately many of our local Christian communities continue in this kind of brain-denying spirituality. Such spirituality may seem pious at first; however, it collapses in the face of any thoughtful person. Unless we only want to be Christians without brains – people who are unable to love God with their minds – our local communities will have to take seriously an intellectually rigorous faith and an intellectually rigorous and compassionate reading of the Bible.

A primary habit of formation is the habit of prayer. Prayer is the spirit in which we are sent. Not prayer simply as a self-indulgent exercise, but prayer as outlined in our discussion in Chapter four in the widest sense of the word *ora*. In fact, one of the basic dimensions of being sent – being apostolic – is to be sent to pray. To be sent grows out of the act of worship and prayer, it is the culmination of worship, and it is the crown of every gathering of Christians. In Matthew we are told that the disciples worshipped Jesus, and then they were sent (Mt. 28:17). It is all the more instructive and comforting to know that this worship was not a self-assured and self-congratulatory worship, because the text adds the striking phrase, "…even though some of them doubted."

The Sacramental Mission of the Local Christian Community

The view from the hill was spectacular. Below us stretched the city of Matanzas, Cuba, with a great Fort punctuating it on the edge of the Caribbean Sea. At our feet lay an organic garden sprouting lettuce, tomatoes, zucchinis, beans and many lush growing vegetables. On our right lay the Chapel of the *Semminario Evangelico de Teologia*. This ecumenical seminary has thrived through thick and thin in Cuba and embodies so much of what we have explored about theological formation above. We had brought theological students from Canada to experience faith in action in an environment diametrically opposite to the consumer culture they are used to. They have come to be formed on the journey.

It is essential to have concrete examples, visible signs – sacramental examples – of God's invisible grace, as points of reference as we think of making real the theological reflection we have done so far. When we consider the *Seminario Evagelico* as a case in point, we can simply begin with the community garden. Food is not only produced for the seminary itself, but it is part of the seminary engagement with the community around it. Like the medieval monasteries of old, food is being shared with those on the margins and its place and role in the work and prayer of the learning community is critical. The garden – representing how we tend and care for God's creation – sits right beside the chapel where the work of prayer and worship is engaged. Sometimes the garden is physically carried into worship as I experienced the one morning during the chapel time when students brought leaves into worship to help the worshippers focus on the wonder of creation. This local community in the shape of the seminary teaches people to raise pigs, to do organic gardening, to develop ways of sustaining themselves in ever more difficult economic circumstances. In addition it creates beauty. Plants are not just to feed but also to flower. Every week children from the community are brought together to dance and to sing, and every Wednesday night Prof. Castellanos-Morente (now sadly deceased), used to lead the whole community in dance. In all these ways this community raise physical signs of the coming reign of God. The sacramental presence forms the participants to continue wherever they go in the same spirit and commitment.

The Local Christian Community – Sent to Call and Sent to Listen

If we live before God as an institution then we find our meaning and purpose in life by being addressed by God. The local Christian community as seminary and all its structures and departments are thus to be focused on the process of listening for the voice of God and hearing God. We are there to hear the call. We are also there to extend God's call to one another and all others. Thus committed and thus sent we are shaped for Christian Spirituality by the dual movements of hearing the call and listening, and extending the call and inviting to listen.

The great narrative of covenant is the rubric under which we listen and hear God's call. N.T. Wright's formulation, "God's plan through Abraham and his family for the world", is a fine formulation of the covenantal narrative that shapes our understanding of our call. Thus we are addressed by God. Like Abraham and Sarah we are barren to be addressed and to be made fruitful through the covenantal call of God. What we hear is a call to renunciation – repentance – turning to a new journey. What we hear then, is the call to mortification (loving self-giving sacrifice), the first movement of the spiritual journey. As we listen in mission this is what we hear:

We hear that our well-being is a gift that grows out of repentance and our well-being is intended to bless all people and creation. We hear God's judgement on us as rebels and we hear God's call for us to return. We hear Genesis 3:9 – God's empassioned call to us – "Where?" echoing through the ages. We hear the judgement of the Messiah pronounced over us, "accepted and free". Paul Tillich put this idea strikingly in his famous sermon, "You Are Accepted."[3]   It is a sermon well worth reading over and over again. We also hear this judgement as invitation on the journey to live out of that judgement as we work out our salvation in fear and trembling in the diverse reality that is God's rich creation. As I argued in Chapter two, following Harold Wells, formation for Christian spirituality has in this way to be specifically centered in Christ. He is the Judge and Saviour and formation is only Christian formation if this unique Christic quality of our understanding remains a constant point of reference. What is important here is to understand that all the matters outline above are to shape the whole of the local Christian community and community in mission.

In Chapter two, following N.T. Wright, we linked diversity to listening. His point being that the very shape of the Pauline epistles suggest that the call to honour and respect diversity within community is integral to the Gospel itself. Most succinctly this is captured in the idea that there is no longer slave nor free, male or female, Jew or Gentile. When people from such diversity gather together in a community of faith their very togetherness witnesses to the Gospel. Hearing the call to diversity is thus not an optional extra as we listen. Hearing and then embracing diversity is the task of the Gospel and the sign that God's reign has come. The local Christian community as seminary is thus by definition to be a place where diversity is welcomed and cultivated.

Such unity and diversity is only possible in community where and as we live out of the habits that arise out of listening to God's call. Our reflection in Chapter two, based in Romans 12, outlined these habits in terms of covenant faithfulness, living eschatologically – out of the age to come, living sacrificially in love, being transformed in mind and heart, living in worship, embodying faith and exerting ourselves towards the habits of God's reign.

We have also argued, based on the Benedictine tradition, that the movements of prayer and work are the building blocks of the community of formation. These two movements also provide the context of our hearing. There is a way in which the disciplines of prayer and work open our ears to hear. Moreover, the whole world we live in – creation itself – is a grand liturgy before God when our eyes and ears are opened in this way. As with Abraham, the stars become sacramental, and the fields blowing in the wind speak of praise to God. Our imaginations and deepest human experiences bear witness to the beauty of Creation. We see the work of the Spirit even in those not explicitly Christian and we recognise the fruit of the Spirit where present in other religious traditions. Thus, our daily engagement with this world and the way that the community encourages this engagement constitutes a critical part of formation. It is specifically a focus on how the great narratives can inform the most mundane parts of life, the observation of our eyes, and the small connections with others as meaningful that is essential in the liturgy of daily life, and essential to formation. When we enter every day we have in our minds the greeting of the day as a place to be called by God, as a place to listen, as an opportunity to journey to the neighbour and creation, as an occasion to experience God's sacramental presence and as the moment to be sent.

We have argued that listening is rooted in engaging the scriptural text, but hearing it is also a function of engaging our neighbour, the other, and particularly those who are "the least of these" in the world and around us. To hear well we need to move. As we listen for God's call – we discover that God often speaks to us through others, who are sacred messengers – the true definition of angels. When I as an eighteen year old in South Africa met my fellow black citizens and heard their stories, the words of the prophets in the Bible spoke powerfully to me through my encounter with their experience. Within the Christian community both the biblical text and the engagement of the neighbour become non-negotiable parts of listening to God. Without others to rub against, to be challenged and to be encouraged, there is no proper formation for Christian spirituality. As we will see in the next section we discover who we are exactly where we are challenged to journey beyond ourselves. We have been created in the image of God as symbols of community – and without community there is no formation.

Out of this listening disposition which is the second element of worship, grows the power to be transformed by God, and to gain the monastic patience, tenacity and perseverance necessary for formation as journey.

The Local Christian Community as Institution of Journey

I pointed out earlier that the local Christian community is the context in and from which we are sent and formed. The second context of formation is the journey. When we are static and comfortable, when we go to be encouraged but we are not challenged and even goaded by God's Spirit to move, Christian spirituality dwindles and it resists taking form in our lives. The rationale for this has been built throughout the chapters leading up to this point. What is the point of call, if we are not called to action, to go, to journey? What do we listen for if it is not for God's invitation to turn and to journey? Why do the narratives of faith in the Hebrew Scriptures shape themselves around journeys? Why is Jesus described in the Gospels as being on the journey to Jerusalem and the cross? Why does Jesus call his disciples to repent and to follow him? Why are the Pauline letters written on a journey? Why does God move beyond Godself to make creation in an outpouring of love? Why does God so love the cosmos that God chooses to become part of it in the incarnation? These questions lead us to the convincing conclusion that Christian spirituality is never static, is always on the move, is shaped and formed when we journey for and in God's mission.

The long tradition of the pilgrimage for and with Christ (*perigrinatio pro Christi*) is thus the next rubric as the process of worship unfolds the different dimensions of formation for Christian spirituality in mission. First of all, the mission of the community is to accompany each person on a journey towards discovering who they are as people. This means that apprehending a Christian theology of the person is critical for our formation. In our earlier exploration of the theology of the person and identity we drew on the insight that the human being represents in some way the community of God the Trinity who is represented in the metaphor of the community of man and woman. In this community we recognise the sign of the image of God (*Imago Dei*). Moreover, it is in the Messiah, the one who calls the disciples to follow in community and the one human being who lives in covenant faithfulness, that we discern the meaning of who we are. This meaning of the Messiah is discovered in listening to the biblical narrative and in engaging our neighbour and creation through journey. On this journey we do two things. We discover ourselves as participants in the whole of God's creation and the whole of community. We also discover ourselves as "self" with our own uniqueness. These two dimensions create a tension between being together and being self. Bringing together these parts is the task of the Christian community that forms us on the journey. This formation happens when we live in the habits that should now be familiar to us.

- It is when we journey towards others that we are challenged to give of ourselves sacrificially in love and resistance against oppression and injustice.
- It is when we engage others on the journey that we are challenged to live in hope despite disappointment, that is to live eschatologically.
- It is in those character forming encounters with others on the journey that we learn what it is to be transformed in mind.
- It is when we know the presence of God by the Spirit on the journey, or when we have to walk in faith without experience that we are challenged to worship.
- The journey challenges to work hard on the way.
- The journey challenges us to covenant faithfulness.
- On the way we work and pray – *ora et labora.*
- Walking on this journey challenges us to do justice, to create beauty, to witness and to raise signs of the coming reign of God.

To be on this journey is by definition mission, to be sent, to be apostolic. The church that emerges out of this process and that nurtures us is only truly apostolic or missional when it moves in this way.

Finally, as pointed out in Chapter three, the seminary as journey is a journey of mutual discernment. In Chapter three we described the categories of discernment within the community in terms of the habits of community. The local Christian community has its input into our formation for spirituality through the process of mutual discernment.

The time has now come to unpack the discernment of such habits as a missional task in more detail. The categories of discernment based in that discussion was drawn from an exploration of Romans 12. Those same categories will appear below in bold, now organised in terms of the larger themes outlined in this book. First, I want to suggest, that the shape of this book, the shape of worship in the Christian life, provides the broad categories of discernment. Thus we can speak of discernment, theologically, in terms of discerning call, listening, journey, sacrament and sending. Mutual discernment on the way of spirituality is a descriptive task. That means we can describe to one another how we see these tasks of worship and its habits take shape in our lives. This means we will tell each other stories of our lives and mutually affirm what we see and encourage and challenge to what we do not see.

The Missional Task of Discerning Call

"I am called by God," insisted the student. "Who are you to question God's sovereign call? I know that I know that I know God has called me. I will be a minister. You cannot stop me…"

In our individualised and consumer driven culture such conceptions of Christian call is all too familiar. It is the "I and my Jesus" syndrome, or "God told me so." For someone who understands faith as a private matter between them and God, and faith as a cure to meet all their needs, such logic of God's call makes sense. However, when we discern call in the context of Christian community and journey as argued here, such conceptions are not helpful. Yes, God calls, but God calls to community, to mortification and sacrifice, to understanding one's task in terms of going beyond meeting your own selfish needs. God's call inspires awe, makes us hide, and in many cases make us run away. Such an awesome call is not discerned individually only, but as person in community. To use Paul Tillich's argument cited in Chapter three, discernment involves both "being as participation in community" and "being as self." Knowing God's general call as well as our specific task in the reign of God is thus not just something individual, it is something that arises out of our personal discernment in concert with the community.

Discerning the Missional Task of Listening

Local Christian communities provide opportunity to listen to the biblical narrative. But we do not listen to these biblical stories out of our context. The diversity of the community, its different perspectives on what they hear and even the input from others far away in other cultures and communities all help us to listen in a missional way. Where we are able to bring together knowledge of the Scriptures and others in acts of wisdom the listening habit is well displayed. To follow Breuggemann's argument explored in Chapter four, these habits demonstrate obedience. Such acts of wisdom and decision occur where we show the ability to be sensitive to those different from ourselves in culture, gender, sexual orientation, or socio–economic status. The task is demonstrated in the bringing together of reading, reflection and action to guide others from diverse backgrounds by displaying interpersonal skills in leading and giving direction. Where we think evaluatively about Scripture and Christian Traditions, we apply our thought in such a way as to achieve the covenantal aims of building for the reign of God. Where conflict is encountered listening habits are shown in the ability to listen fairly and intervening in constructive ways. Thus the task of listening represents the habit of **covenant faithfulness.**

Discerning the Missional Task of Journey

We can discern, encourage and admonish one another in relation to our willingness to be on the way with the Gospel. Perhaps the most fundamental way this is tested in our local communities is when we are challenged to move beyond our comfort zone. We can also discern this task as we ask ourselves to what extent we take seriously the destruction of our biosphere and our own actions to care for it? When we highlight these elements within our communities we are given the opportunity to discern the missional task of journey – *perigrinatio pro Christi* – in one another. In this journey of engagement our own strengths, gifts and challenges become clear. The journey aids accurate ways of assessing and describing ourselves. Engaging the journey also opens us to hear where others bring compassionate description of their challenges to awareness. The journey exposes us to become aware of boundaries and gives opportunity for us to show our understanding of appropriate boundaries knowing the differentiation between self and the other – difference in the midst of community. Thus respectful engagement of the other and creation is demonstrated and discerned and can be described in terms of concrete action. The journey is both mission in itself and instructor in spirituality. It is on the journey that we build the habits of **self-giving sacrifice** through the mortification of our own self-focused concerns. It is also here, on the journey that the **transformation of the mind** is demonstrated as the journey challenges and stretches us. Moreover, the journey challenges us to **embody** our faith. Perhaps this is what James meant when he wrote, "My answer is, 'Show me how anyone can have faith without actions. I will show you my faith by my actions' (James 2:18)."

Discerning the Missional Task of Sacrament

Sacrament or being sacramental as we understand it here is about being able to make God's reign visible, to enable others to taste, to smell, to chew, to know in an embodied form that grace abounds. How do we see such sacramental habits displayed in our lives? Of course the embodiments of the habits of call, listening and journey are already sacramental in as much as they are shown in the action and engagement of people in community. In Chapter four we have discussed sacrament particularly in relation to the two movements of the monastic and Benedictine tradition of work and prayer. We have also pointed to the idea that work is prayer and prayer is work. The seamless living of prayer and work and its display in personal discipline thus is sacramental. Prayerful study and reflection become observable in a person's ability to bring this learning into integrated wisdom to the community. Thus, it is not so much in overt piety (saying earnest or beautiful prayers or singing beautiful songs, or studying the Bible privately), but rather in piety as right living in community with God that the sacramental task is exposed. Yet, it is also important, I hasten to say, that the sacramental is demonstrated in beauty and creativity. Beautiful prayers and songs, music and all forms of art that invite and mediate communion with one another and God are demonstrations of the sacramental task. Thus working hard at liturgical leadership while considering all those engaged and doing it well, is both work and prayer and an integral part of Christian spirituality. It is not just the task of a few experts, it is the task of all in community to participate and to lead. The Zimbabwean tree planting liturgy cited in Chapter four demonstrates how such beauty and creativity come together with the missional task. In no small way the sacramental habit is demonstrated in being faithful to the overt sacramental life of the Christian community in Baptism and Eucharist. It is therefore in the sacramental task that we demonstrates the habit of **worship in community.**

Discerning the Task of Mission – Being Sent

"The church exists for others", the apostolic or missional task is a demonstration of the "for others" dimension of Christian spirituality. However, the "for others" language could imply a kind of paternalism. A better way to speak of this missional habit is to speak of *being with others* rather than *doing for others*. Such a movement beyond us is not in a form of know-better paternalism, but in service with, among, and in solidarity with those being engaged. This movement beyond us, beyond our comfort zone and despite our personal needs, demonstrates the missional task. In this way we become signs and foretastes of God's coming reign. Such missional habits grow out of the process of call, listening, journeying, and sacramental living. In a real way it demonstrates a response to the injunction of Romans 12:1,

> "offer yourself as a living sacrifice to God dedicated to God's service
> and pleasing to God. This is the true worship you shall offer." (GNB)

The missional task is also **eschatological**, a category of discernment discussed in Chapter three, it demonstrates living in hope when the reign of God is not yet fully come. To act missionally with others requires hope for the coming reign of God that is not yet fully realised.

In the context of the tasks of call, listening, journeying, sacramental living, and sending the spirituality of the coming reign of God is thus both demonstrated and grown in our lives. To be sent is to be sent with and in the church. This church is missional by nature and this is expressed in its dimensions of sacramentality, apostolicity, and presence.

The Sacramental Dimension of the Emerging Missional Church

Not only is the local Christian community as expression of church to be the context of formation for Christian spirituality, but also in a concrete way it is to emerge as a sacramental missional sign in the world. This sacramental missional dimension of church cannot be divorced from spirituality. The local Christian community as the institution of church is to be Christomorphic (shaped like Christ), concretely demonstrating the Spirit of the Messiah in its life, curriculum, and action. It is therefore called to be different, counter cultural, alternative, a sign of the age to come, rather than a sign of the enlightenment soaked, industrial, consumer, digital culture of our time. This does not mean that it should be culturally head in sand, denying the realities wherein it exists, but that it should be sacramental in being bold in challenging all that which is not of the reign of God.

Our discussion in Chapter four particularly attended to Breuggemann's argument for Christian education shaped by the biblical Canon. If one begins there, and with the assumption of Canon or Scripture one is already countercultural. What this means is that the local Christian community, as institution in the world, exists to be addressed by God first. It is there to listen corporately and to respond. We can speak of a corporate spirituality expressed in the community and institution. God and God's texts are not our object. God addresses us, calls us into being and constitutes us. We read the texts of the Hebrew and Greek Scriptures as Scripture rather than simply as book. We read first to be spoken to not to critique. This does not mean that we do not engage critical scholarship, biblical criticism, insights from cultural tradition and archaeological research and so on. We do and we must, but we do so knowing that we cannot do so from a place of arrogance. We are creatures in God's creation – God is not our creation and neither are the ancient texts of communities of faith simply our academic game. Here God is always addressed as Thou in awe and we are, as Breuggemann points out, called to obey. Such a disposition is counter cultural and is a visible sign of God's reign – a visible sign of invisible grace.

As a *visible* sign, the community and institution is decidedly not a place for other-worldly piety. It is not a place of escape, but a place for concrete engagement with God's creatures and God's creation. Matter matters. And the appearance of our institutions in buildings and organisation matters. Where the local Christian community takes on the shape of pragmatic business practice it loses its ability to be sacramental and missional. We are to be communities of extra measure of grace, communities that walk a second mile, and communities that seek biblical justice not the revenge of a "justice system". We are to be inclusive, slow when we have to slow down with those challenged physically and mentally, and poor where being rich reflects the exploitation of others. Our fellow community members are not objects, vehicles or conveniences; they are certainly not objects of our judgment; they are people to be respected as carrying the image of God. Even where they are angry, nasty, and arrogant, we shall seek to love, forgive and heal. It is in this way God's grace is made visible. Not only matter matters, but also our canon law, rule books, or polity and the way we deal with one another. In the difference of these things from the ways of the present age the emerging missional church is to represent its corporate spirituality.

The Local Christian Community and the Emerging Missional Church as institution of Sending – a truly Apostolic Institution

Soon after the early church became acceptable within the Roman Empire, the occurrence of so called "red martyrdom" declined. "Red martyrdom" was the name early Christians gave to the reality that those who bore witness for the Gospel were persecuted, tortured and killed. In its place came the commitment of "white martyrdom" or "white witness." This was the witness of lives completely dedicated and given to God and God's reign. Saint Columba's early monastery and seminary on the island of Iona was no stranger to red martyrdom, but it was in the first place an institution of sending of Christian leaders who had given their lives completely as living sacrifices in love to bear witness to the Gospel to the Scots and Picts. The overwhelming task before those early monks was no smaller than that before local Christian communities and the church today. Communities that will have the strength to meet boldly the forces of our time can do well by learning from these ancient institutions such as the Iona community monastery of Columba. In addition, the new Iona of today, as a new monastic community embodies the qualities of an institution living out of the age to come described above. To be sent, the church has to become to some degree an inside out institution[4]. Local Christian communities exist to send people away, yet to support them on the way. As the disciples spent time with Jesus until they were sent out in the sign and Spirit of the Messiah, so local Christian communities are to spend time together to enable us to leave and to fulfill God's call in our lives. Thus local Christian communities are also to emerge as pilgrim institutions.

The Gospel of John presents a different story from the Synoptic Gospels of the sending of the disciples. In it Jesus appears to the disciples in a locked room, greets them with peace, breathes on them invoking the coming of the Holy Spirit, and then sends them with the words, "As the Father sent me so I am sending you..." Sending or mission then, seen from John's perspective, is at its heart Christomorphic. It is to be sent as Christ, the Messiah was sent. It is to go as Christ went. It is to teach as Christ taught, and it is in turn to send others as Christ sent. Yet the presence of the Spirit and the promise, earlier in the Gospel, of the other Counsellor that will come to the disciples also imply an ongoing connection and mentoring relationship. As sending institution the local Christian community thus maintains a responsibility of mentorship, encouragement, and invitation. That is, if it wishes to reflect sending as Jesus sent!

The word *alumnus* literally means to be a nursling! Perhaps this should suggest a transformed understanding of what the relationship is between the seedbed – the local community as seminary – and the nursling – *alumnus*. Can we envisage our local Christian communities as sending institutions who take responsibility and share vows together? What would happen if local Christian communities thought of themselves in the same way as the contemporary way of the Iona community in Scotland? Members of such a community can have different levels of membership but such membership requires vows to mutual responsibility, contributing to the good the community, and committing to certain disciplines, and of course, mutual support.

The Local Christian Community as Institution of Presence in our Time and Context

Does the argument above appear idealistic? Of course no institution will completely fulfil these habits and rubrics; neither would participants neatly fall into categories. We live in a broken and warped world and the church is as much part of this state as any other institution. In fact bureaucratising systems will always remain a challenge in any institution, perhaps a necessary evil to live with? However, the greater challenge local Christian communities and larger church institutions face in implementing its task of formation has been hinted at several times so far. Culture and context in North America and globally has gone through momentous change over the last fourty years. Theological study and research often rely heavily on internet resources and sometimes succumb to the great "copy and paste" temptation of the internet. New church members come expecting the local congregation to tailor things to their needs. A consumer disposition expects the institution to adapt programs, and meeting times to their personal preferences. In fact some schools of thought call this "seeker sensitive" church.

Beyond these obvious and radical changes to the environment of formation is a change in attitude and consciousness within culture. This is a much more subtle change. Within the local Christian community today we have not only different cultures from different continents (particularly in urban Canada); we also have different generational cultures. There is a wide stretch in age between younger and older members we also have a very wide gap in the way the world is perceived and engaged. There is a process on the go of a radical reshaping of consciousness. I have discussed this matter in greater detail elsewhere, but here I would like to outline a few of the salient issues relevant to formation for spirituality[5].

Perhaps the most interesting change in younger generations is a shift from a present consciousness to a future consciousness. Shaped by a consumer and technological culture that is driven by everything that is new and improved in technology, we live in a constant expectation that something better will come next year. On a surface level this is represented in the newest iPhone or iPad, Samsung, or Blackberry, but on a deeper level it represents an attitude that the new is better than the old. The importance of history, grasping the roots of things, knowing origins and so on become largely irrelevant to a person shaped by a future-consciousness. In this mode, identity is not something gained from heritage, reflection and insight; identity becomes something to be invented and reinvented, and even changed over time. According to the argument made in this book, it will be clear that such future-consciousness risks understanding our place in the great narrative of God and might miss the insight offered by experiences and theological reflections through history. The church itself, as it draws on its rich traditions, is thus in a very basic way counter-cultural. The assumptions of social networking, texting and tweeting, are also challenged to some degree with the emphasis on authentic presence, and learning through encounter with others in community. Part of our problem is the way that traditional conceptions of local Christian communities are still shaped by the print medium. Biblical arguments, exploring Christian traditions, and literary study, are all based in the assumption of Guttenberg. In contrast new generations are steeped in the assumptions of Bill Gates and Steve Jobs. It is easy to react to these differences in dismay! Does this make the task impossible?

Absolutely not! If we follow the logic of the argument we have made so far we must first of all affirm that difference in our community and difference in culture (or sub-culture) is not a bane but a blessing to be embraced as part of the Gospel itself. Every person, no matter how different, is created in the image of God for community. Each has a valid perspective to bring. They are called as all are called, their journeys are as important as ours and their insights will be gained through their own processes. The 'otherness' within our communities is not a problem but a gift.

Let us take "digital community" as an example. It is easy to play on the sentiment that people who connect via digital networking or text messaging are not really in community with one another. However, the generations raised on the telephone do not always see how the phone has changed their perceptions of connection and community. Over thirty years that I have spent in ministry, I have seen the phone, telephone conferencing, and cell-phones radically change how I connect with people. This has not always been a bad thing. Presently, I am becoming aware how recent graduates from my College connect with one another through social media. In the vast geography of Canada, they seem to have a constant awareness of one another and their activities stretched thousands of kilometres apart. Subtle signals sent in a more public way often lead to more personal telephone interactions where mutual support is required. Without a doubt the ways of building local Christian communities are also changing with these technologies in our North American context. Creative ways of enhancing community with and not against such technologies is thus an essential part of the formation for spirituality, institutional integrity and mission.

The cultural consciousness is also shifting to an interactive stance rather than a passive observer stance[6]. Interactivity, requires mutual engagement. Much of regular church life in the North American context has been decidedly passive based in the observer habits of television watchers. Today, our leaders face the opportunity to transform worship and community into places of authentic interaction and dialogue, rather than passive – sit in the pew – observation. If journey in the Christian life is as important as I argue in this book, then this provides for ways to invite people to move, to journey, to go, to discover Bunyan's "avowed intent to be a pilgrim."

None of this means that there are not things to challenge and question and oppose in our consumer digital culture in North America.   There are many such things including information inflation without wisdom, the false sense of anonymity created by the internet and digital media that ruptures mutual responsibility and community, the temptations of internet addictions, and so on. Most of all, to be unaware of how these new technologies shape and use us is to be deeply naïve[7]. However, they are part of the world we live in, they are shaping us, and we need to engage this reality with faith grounded in God's great narrative of creation and redemption. That is our mission.

Conclusion

In this chapter we have followed the final logic of the structure of worship. We are sent into the world to build for and with the reign of God. We are to be missional. We have explored what this means for the formation of Christian spirituality in the local Christian community and within the larger institution of the church that is emerging in our time. We have seen how this missional dimension captures and integrates all the elements of worship and displays God's great narrative of creation and redemption. We have also seen how the local Christian community is to be by its nature missional and is to stand sacramentally in a missional relationship with its alumni. It is to give expression to a corporate Christian spirituality in the world. We are to be like the white monastery, institutions that send people into the world to bear costly witness. This witness occurs in the context of the consumer, technological, digital culture of our time. It is a challenging task but one from which we dare not shrink back.

Notes

1. The Nicene–Constantinopolitan Creed.

2. Butler, K. "The Anatomy of Resilience; New Research Shows What Helps People Shake Off Adversity." *The Family Therapy Networker* (21:1) March/April 1997.

3. Tillich, Paul, *The Shaking of the Foundations.* New York:C. Scribner's Sons. 1948 150-164.

4. Hoekendijk, J.C. *The Church Inside Out.* London: SCM Press, 1967.

5. Fensham, C.J. *Emerging from the Dark Age Ahead: The Future of the North American Church.* Toronto: Clements Academic, 2011.

6. Ibid. 97-101

7. Marshall McLuhan coined his famous "McLuhanism" "We shape our tools and thereafter they shape us" in 1964.

Postlude

According to Luke the Apostle Paul instructed the religious investigators of the Areopagus by insisting that we live and move and have our being in God (Acts 17:28). Epimenides' (the 6th century BC philosopher poet from Crete) great poem thus found its way into the Christian Scriptures and echoes the argument of this book. To say that we live and move and have our being in God is another way of saying that we live in the great story of God and creation. God is not just the impassable God – the God who cannot feel our struggle and pain. God is not the God of the Greek philosophers. We are in a very real sense in God who is empassioned by our plight as creatures. We are in God who is in love with us and creation. God has loved so that God made room for creation. God the Room-Maker, the one who is Hospitality-in-Being and Community-in-Relationship, encompasses us yet also lets us live and move thus giving us freedom. We ponder this as we consider our sending and our going in Christian spirituality.

In the small shape of weekly or daily worship the postlude gives us an opportunity to gather our thoughts and to muster our energies for the task ahead. In this small shape of weekly worship discipline we prepare for the large shape of the liturgy of life and relationships that we enter every day. Postludes are not optional; they are essential moments to steel ourselves for the task ahead. Like the disciples locked and afraid in the upper room, we need to let sink in those words of the risen Messiah, "peace be with you – shalom". In the rhythm of prayer and work and work and prayer, the moments of gathering our thoughts and experiences, and letting the Call of God – the hearing of God's Word – sink in are critical to the task ahead.

We receive peace. The assurance of the Spirit of peace is infused in us. Then we, in the way of God the Messiah, go. "As the Father sent me so send I you." This is tough, yet it is the most natural thing in the world. For us to engage God's creation as caregivers and healers – cosmic healers – is to become who we truly are. It is to re-inhabit our being. For all these reasons all Christian spirituality and all forms of Christian formation can only be healthy, integral, and true to our created purpose if we live out of this great story of God's creation and our rightful place in it.

As we ponder the command to go. As we ponder obedience to God. It is good to recall the unfolding experience of worship as it forms us for our task as creatures in God's creation. Worship tells the great story of God and God's creation. More than tell, it is in awe of it and praise God for it! In this book we have followed the traditions of worship in call, listening, journeying, sacrament and sending. We have traced the habits of Christian spirituality. Now, in the postlude we gather these meditations and their implications for us.

We are all **called**. Our calling is first to the ancient covenant of creation in which we are people together as image of God in our communion. We are created to be fellows. We are called into being by God and shaped by the Breath of God that animates us. We are part of creation but also placed in it with caring responsibility. This means that we are not called for something disembodied, ethereal, and other-worldly; our calling is for this world and for its healing transformation which we come to know as the coming reign of God. Our calling is to be and to become community in communion with God's creation. We are formed within this larger shape of God's unfolding purpose. We go in the sign of world-repair.

Formation for Christian spirituality is thus to be a formation in body and in community, a calling to live concretely and to understand our worship, prayer, and work as a function of God's beloved creation. Our local communities and our institutions of formation are thus to embody and value the concrete engagement of the creation and the other.

We hear the agonising call of God the Creator to hiding and rebelling human beings. This too is part of our formational call. We are called back to God. We are to return, repent, so that we as humankind and all things in creation can be brought back to God. Our return is crucial to the healing and transformation of creation. God is a God of social communion and creation itself is being invited into communion with God.

We hear and contemplate God's call to Abraham. This is the great covenant call to world repair. Abraham, Sarah and their family are blessed that all may be blessed. Yet, the blessing proceeds from God, all the promises come from God and eventually covenant faithfulness on the human side come from God through the Messiah. God's promise to Abraham, "I will bless you and make your name famous, so that you will be a blessing" (Gen 2:2 GNB), through the Messiah, extends to all people. In this moment of postlude, we ponder the call to become a blessing, world-repairers, earth caregivers, to all creation and all things. God's great story of creation is thus a story of cosmic redemption of which we are a part.

To be formed for Christian spirituality is to be formed within hearing this Abrahamic call and its appeal to us. It is to leave behind our own Babylon and to journey to the other, the stranger, the marginalised – the unknown and yet partly unrealised land of God's redemption.

As we consider the process of the worship of God that we have explored in this book we **listen**. Postludes invite us to consider what we have heard. We have heard of the habits of covenant faithfulness. This includes covenant faithfulness, eschatological living, sacrificial self-giving, the transformation of the mind, living in our bodies, worship in the Benedictine shape of work and prayer, and working hard on the way. Formation for Christian leadership invites us to these habits and discerns them in our lives.

We reflect on how our identity becomes clear to us on a **journey**. God journeys with creation and so do we. As Abraham and Sarah journeyed and passed through many ups and downs, so we too engage the journey expecting that our destiny and meaning as people will become clear. Who we are as human beings and why and to what end we exist becomes apparent on the journey with God. We walk in the ancient Celtic tradition of the *perigrinatio pro Christi*. Because the Messiah is the one that walks with us, our journey is in the form of the journey of Christ. We are to have a christomorphic journey together. This journey shapes us in the habits of spirituality. On this way we live in the tension between participating in community and being as self. Our engagement with hearing God's word to us is enhanced and amplified in our engagement with our neighbours, the marginalised, the suffering, and all creation. When we feed them we obey and love God. This is the journey towards justice and beauty.

Formation for this journey is to be in the sign of the tradition of "white witness" or "white martyrdom", the giving of ourselves completely to God. This is mortification which leads to life. Dietrich Bonhoeffer's wise counsel that the call to discipleship is the call to die, is to be treasured in the light of the wisdom of the Gospel that losing your life is finding it. Discerning such commitment is a tenuous task.

We ponder the **sacramental** nature of our call. Together as community we are to be in the image of God. We are to be signs of the reign of God on earth. This sign is lived in the loving logic of worship with prayer and work. Our work implies effort and commitment. As we exert ourselves to live the life of God's reign we realise that this effort and exertion is the product of God's grace. It is by the Spirit of the Messiah that we are enabled to live as signs of God's coming reign. Such sacramental living means that God's reign can be seen, tasted, and experienced. To such living we are called.

Formation for sacramental journey involves a commitment to the sacramental life of worship as well as to the sacramental sign-like living in community in the world. Our living is to bear witness. Such living is evangelism.

We consider our state of being sent by God. Come wind, come weather we are being sent. Together we are marked by being an apostolic people. The postlude gives us time to reflect on being sent. We are not sent as isolated individuals, we are sent as communities of faith. We are sent together. Formation for our mission takes place in our local community as it demonstrates its commitment to God's mission. Our institutions of formation are to be examples or demonstrations – signs of God's mission in and with creation. Such a mission has to engage the complex and challenging structure of every context. In the North American and Canadian context this means engaging a commoditised consumer culture in a digital environment. Formation in this context challenges us to form people for community against the pressures of isolation and anonymity. It also challenges us to invite those being formed to seek wisdom rather than mere information or data.

The task is hard; it is martyr work – the work of Christian witness. In the mad rush of the contemporary consumer and digital world we live with many demands on our time. The call of the cultural matrix is to perform, not to have time for others, to produce things so that we can consume more or impress others, rather than to walk with one another in relationship. For the Christian leader the challenge is that the Gospel call, the Call of the Messiah, and the Call of the Creator calls us to grow ourselves and our communities in a different direction. We are called to engage others, to have time, to care, gather, embrace, and share. We are called as cosmic healers, we are called to do justice, love mercy, and walk humbly. This is hard because it is counter cultural. "I cannot see you because I am too busy" is the prime excuse of our culture. Somehow being busy has gained false virtue.

Postludes help us ponder how we shall counter the demands of false virtues as we go. They provide us with psychological space to be grasped by the transformative moral vision of the story of God and God's creation. In his 1979 reflection on the postlude James Heynan claimed two very important things about the postlude and its place in communal worship. First he claims that it should provide a bridge from our communal worship to the world we have to live in. It is therefore the bridge from ora to labora, from prayer to work. Secondly, the postlude should facilitate obedience because God is not truly worshipped until we obey.[1] If Christian spirituality is the spirituality of the road, spirituality only truly lived on a journey, then, the postlude and these last thoughts are to give us courage to go on the journey with God. Now we shall cross the bridge...

Notes

1. http://www.calvin.edu/worship/lit_arts/music/brink_heynen.php (Accessed August 11, 2010).

Bibliography

Bibliography

Anderson, E & Valpy, M (Eds.). *The New Canada: A Globe and Mail Report on the Next Generation.* Toronto: McClelland and Stewart, 2004.

Barth, K. *Church Dogmatics III, 2: The Doctrine of Creation.* Edinburgh: T. & T. Clark, 1960.

—. *Church Dogmatics III, I.* London: T & T Clark, 1977.

—. *Church Dogmatics IV, 2: The Doctrine of Reconciliation.* Edinburgh: T. & T. Clark, 1996.

—. *The Epistle to the Romans.* Oxford: Oxford University Press, 1968.

Bevans, S.B. & Schroeder, R.P. *Constants in Context: A Theology of Mission for Today.* New York: Orbis Press, 2004.

Bibby, Reginald. *Restless Churches.* Ottawa: Novalis, 2004.

—. "Restless Gods and Restless Youth: An Update on the Religious Situation in Canada." *Presented at the Annual Meeting of the Canadian Sociological Association.* Ottawa: http://www.reginaldbibby.com/images/Revision_Bibby_CSA_Presentation,_Ottawa_May_09.pdf (Accessed December 29, 2009), 2009. 1-14.

Bonhoeffer, D. *The Cost of Discipleship.* London: SCM/Canterbury Press, 2001.

Bosch, D.J. *A Spirituality of The Road.* Eugene: Wipf and Stock, 2001.

– "The Church in South Africa – Tomorrow." *Theologia Evangelica,* 1976: 171-186.

– *Transforming Mission: Paradigm Shifts in Theology of Mission.* New York: Orbis, 1991.

Bramadat, Paul and Seljak, David (Eds.). *Christianity and Ethnicity in Canada.* Toronto: University of Toronto Press, 2008.

Breuggemann, W. *Genesis – Interpretation: A Bible Commentary for Teaching and Preaching.* Atlanta: John Knox Press, 1982.

—. *The Creative Word: Canon as Model for Biblical Education.* Philadelphia: Fortress Press, 1982.

Brown, Callum G. *The Death of Christian Britain: Understanding Secularization 1800-2000.* New York: Routledge, 2001.

Brown, P. *Augustine of Hippo: A Biography.* Berkley: University of California Press, 1969.

Bruce, Steve. *God is Dead: Secularization in the West.* Oxford: Blackwell, 2002.

Butler, Judith *Bodies That Matter: On the Discursive Limits of Sex.* New York: Routledge, 1993.

Calvin, J. (Translated by H. Beverage). *The Institutes of the Christian Religions Book IV.* Grand Rapids: William B. Eerdmans Publishing Company, 1957.

Critchley, Simon & Bernasconi, Robert (Eds.) *The Cambridge Companion to Levinas.* Cambridge: Cambridge University Press, 2002.

Dawn, M. *Reaching Out Without Dumbing Down: A Theology of Worship for This Urgent Time.* Grand Rapids: William B. Eerdmans Publishing Company, 1995.

Dulles, Avery R. *Models of the Church.* New York: Double Day Books, 1991.

Fensham, Charles James. *Emerging From the Dark Age Ahead: The Future of the North American Church.* Toronto: Clements Academic, 2011.

Finke, Rodger and Stark, Rodney. *The Churching of America 1776-1990.* New Brunswick: Rutgers, 1992.

Fretheim, Terence E. *God and the World in the Old Testament: A Relational Theology of Creation.* Nashville: Abingdon Press.

Gilligan, Carol. *In A Different Voice: Psychological Theory and Women's Development.* Harvard: Harvard University Press, 1982.

Goheen, M. *"As the Father Has Sent Me, I am Sending You" J.E. Lesslie Newbigin's Missionary Ecclesiology.* Utrecht: Die Boekencentrum, 2000.

Guder, Darrell L. *The Continuing Conversion of the North American Church.* Grand Rapids: Eerdmans, 2000.

Hall, Douglas John. *The End of Christendom and the Future of Christianity.* Eugene Or.: Wipf and Stock, 1997.

Hauerwas, Stanley. "The Servant Community: Christian Social Ethics." In *The Hauerwas Reader,* by Berkmann, J. & Cartwright M. (Eds.). Durham: Duke University Press, 2003.

Hirsch, A. *The Forgotten Ways: Reactivating the Missional Church.* Grand Rapids: William B. Eerdmans Publishing Company, 2006.

Illich, Ivan. *The Church, Change and Development.* Chicago: Urban Development Center, 1970.

Jacobs, Jane. *Dark Age Ahead.* New York: Random House, 2004.

Kearney, R. *The God who May Be.* Bloomington: Indianna University Press, 2001.

Kearney, Richard. *On Stories.* New York: Routledge Press, 2002.

Lee, J.G. *Celebrating God's Cosmic Perichoresis: The Eschatologial Panentheim of Jurgen Moltmann as a Resource for and Ecological Christian Worhip.* Toronto: Th.D. Thesis, Knox College, University of Toronto, 2009.

Levinas, E. (Translated by Smith, M.B. & Harshaw, B.). *On Thinking-of-the-Other Entre Nous.* New York: Columbia University Press, 1998.

Levinson, Daniel J. *The Seasons of a Man's Life.* New York: Random House, 1978.

Lyon, David & Van Die, Marguerite (Eds.). *Rethinking Church, State and Modernity: Canada between Europe and America.* Toronto: University of Toronto Press, 2000.

Lyon, David. "Introduction." In *Rethinking Church, State and Modernity: Canada between Europe and America,* by David Lyon and Marguerite van Die, 1-19. Toronto: University of Toronto Press, 2000.

Macdonald, Stuart. ""Death of Christian Canada? Do Canadian church statistics support Callum Brown's timing of church decline?" ." *Canadian Society of Church History.* Canadian Society for Church History, 2006.

Macdonald, Stuart. "Religion and Secularization in Canada: Education and the Impact on Mission." In *Christian Mission and Education in Modern China, Japan, and Korea: Historical Studies,* by J.A.B. Jongeneel, P.T.M. Ng, C.K. Paek, S.W. Sunquist and Y. Watanabe, 27-35. New York: Peter Lang, 2009.

Martin, David. "Canada in Comparative Perspective." In *Rethinking Church, State and Modernity: Canada between Europe and America,* by David Lyon and Margaret Van Die (Eds.). Toronto: University of Toronto Press, 2000.

McCarroll, Pamela. *Waiting for the Thief in the Night: The Character of Christian Hope in the Theology of the Cross for the North American Context.* Toronto: Ph.D.l Thesis: University of Saint Michael's College, 2006.

McFague. Sally *The Body of God: An Ecological Theology.* Minneapolis: Fortress Press.

Milavic, A. *The Didache: Text Translation, Analysis, and Commentary.* Collegeville: Liturgical Press, 2003.

Miller, M. Rex. *The Millennium Matrix: Reclaiming the Past, Reframing the Future, of the Church.* San Fancisco: Jossey-Bass, 2004.

Moltmann, Jürgen *The Theology of Hope: On the Ground and the Implications of Christian Eschatology.* New York: Harper Row, Publishers, 1967.

__. *God in Creation.* New York: Harper Row, 1985.

__. *The Church in the Power of the Spirit: A Contribution to Messianic Ecclesiology.* Minneapolis: Fortress Press, 1993.

__. *The Crucified God*. Minneapolis: Fortress Press, 1993.

__. *The Crucified God: The Cross of Christ as the Foundation and Criticism of Christian Theology*. Minneapolis: Fortress Press, 1993.

__. *Experiences in Theology*. Minneapolis: Fortress Press, 2000.

Moo, D.J. *The Epistle to the Romans*. Grand Rapids: William B. Eerdmans Publishing Company, 1996.

Nevitte, Neil. *The Decline of Deference*. Peterborough, On.: Broadview Press, 1996.

Newbigin, J.E.L. *The Household of God: Lectures on the Nature of the Church*. London: SCM, 1953.

Platcher, William C. *Callings: Twenty Centuries of Christian Vocation*. Grand Rapids: William B. Eerdmans Publishing Company, 2005.

Postman, N. *Technopoly: The Surrender of Culture to Technology*. New York: Alfred A. Knopf, 1992.

Purves, A. *Pastoral Theology in the Classical Tradition*. Knoxville: Westminster/John Knox Press, 2001.

Roof, Wade Clark. *Spiritual Marketplace: baby boomers and the remaking of American Religion*. Princeton: Princeton University Press, 1999.

Sailhammer, J.H. *The Pentateuch as Narrative: A Biblical-Theological Commentary*. Grand Rapids: Zondervan, 1992.

Sanders, E.P. *Paul and Palestinian Judaism: A Comparison of Patterns of Religion*. London: SCM Press, 1977.

—. *Paul: A Very Short Introduction*. Oxford: Oxford University Press, 2001.

Schutz, Paul. *Zwischen Nil und Kaukasus: ein Reisebericht zur religionspolitischen Lage im Orient*. Munchen: Kassell, 1930.

Stone, Bryan. *Evangelism after Christendom: The Practice of Christian Witness*. Grand Rapids: Brazos Press, 2007.

Swimme, Brian *The Universe Story: From the Primordial Flaring Forth to the Ecozoic Era: A Celebration of the Unfolding of the Cosmos*. New York: Harper Collins, 1994.

Taylor, Charles. *A Secular Age*. Harvard: Harvard University Press, 2007.

The Presbyterian Church in Canada. *The Book of Praise*. Montreal: The Presbyterian Church in Canada, 1997.

Tillich, P. *Systematic Theology: Volume 1. Reason and Revelation, Being and God*. Chicago: Chicago University Press, 1951.

—. *The Courage to Be*. New Haven: Yale University Press, 1952.

Ukpong, J. "Essay in Inculturation Biblical Hermeneutic." *Semeia* (73, 2000) 189-210.

van Selms, A. *De Prediking van het Oude Testament: Genesis Deel 1.* Nijkerk: Uit-geverij G.F. Callenbach, 1967.

Vanderburg, Willem H. *Living in the Labyrinth of Technology.* Toronto: University of Toronto Press, 2005.

Volf, Miroslav. *After our Likeness: The Church in the Image of the Trinity.* Grand Rapids: Eerdmans, 1998.

Von Allmen, D. "The Birth of Theology: Contextualization as the Dynamic Element in the Formation of New Testament Theology." *The International Review of Mission*, no. 44:253 (1975): 37-55.

Von Rad, G. *Old Testament Theology Volume I.* New York: Harper Rowe, 1962.

Wells, H. *The Christic Center: Life-Giving and Liberating.* New York: Orbis Books, 2004.

Wenham, G.J. *Word Biblical Commentary. Genesis 1-15.* Nashville: Thomas Nelson, 1978.

Wilson Hargrove, Jonathan. *New Monasticism: What it has to say to today's churches.* Grand Rapids: Brazos Press, 2008.

Wright, N.T. *Justification.* Downers Grove: Intervarsity Press, 2009.

—. *Paul for Everyone: Romans: Part II: Chapters 9-16.* Louisville: Westminster/John Knox Press, 2004.

—. *Surprised by Hope: Rethinking Heaven, The Resurrection, and the Mission of the Church.* New York: Harper One, 2008.

CPSIA information can be obtained at www.ICGtesting.com
Printed in the USA
LVOW10s0409111014

408253LV00003B/58/P